WINE MADE EASY

WINE MADE EASY

by

Gianluca Rottura

ISBN 1-58961-168-3

Published by PageFree Publishing, Inc.
109 South Farmer Street
Otsego, MI 49078
www.pagefreepublishing.com

Contents

ACKNOWLEDGEMENTS

First and Foremost, I would like to thank all my customers
for their trust and continued support.
Next, I would like to thank all of those who have brought us so many great wines.
(In No Particular Order)

Andrea, Mrs Englisis, Spyros, Arnaud, Cathy, John, Nick, Dan, Barbara, Bartolo, Sheila, Willie, Tad, Gaston, Camillo, Roc, Francesco, Livio, Elmer, Irv, Jerry, Suzette, Jim, Violante, Violante Jr., Bill, Luca, Peter, Marty, Spiritoso, Tarallo, Luis, Diego, Nicola, Marco, Jan, Phil, Maurizio, Luigi, Adam, Patrick.

Third, I would like to thank my family, friends, and of course wine staff.
Gianbruno, Carlos, Fernando, Eladio, Ma, Papa.
Extra Special Thanks to:

All the teachers who told me I was wrong, stupid, and hopeless.
For all the times I was thrown out of the classrooms just for disagreeing.
Passing off the required low grades to me to help fill your quotas.
To every other person who doubted me.

P.S. I wrote a book to make you look.

INTRODUCTION

IN this day and age, anyone can write a book on anything. Go to a bookstore and have yourself a laugh. There are books ranging from "How to match your socks and Tupper Ware" to "How to sue companies that make you fat." The books written on wine are more than numerous. Some are fantastic and very informative. Others are average, but hey what can you do. Wine is a real hard topic to cover. That is why I decided to summarize everything. More importantly I added a little advice here and there. The advice you may ignore if you wish, but the rest are good facts you should know.

While writing this book, a friend asked, "Well, what makes you qualified to write a book?" I was surprised he would ask me that. I thought he would put 2 and 2 together. He is a friend and does know who I am, but you the reader probably do not. So it is only fair that you ask, "Hey buddy, what makes you qualified to write a book, heh?"

I was born and raised in New York City to Italian immigrants. I was raised in a very old fashioned household and the Italian culture played a big role in my life. I drank wine when I was just a toddler. I remember telling my elementary school teachers that I drank wine at dinner. I watched them go nuts. "What do you mean wine at dinner? You're only six," they yelled. I responded, "Look. Relax. It's better than a cup of milk. And besides peanut butter sandwiches are not considered dinner at my house." Dinner at my house was a feast. I was not like the other kids. I loved eating all kinds of vegetables. I ate things that are now considered delicacies that would make a kid (and some adults) throw up. At an early age, I was pairing wine with food. It was just a natural thing for me. When I would go to Italy, I would watch my relatives work in the vineyards.

Back home in New York City, my father had a very successful Italian restaurant. I learned the business, which is not as glamorous as most people think. By age 18, my brother and I were running our family's own wine shop. Together we tasted thousands of wines and began learning more than ever. We went to almost every tasting there was and read a lot of books. I always wanted to write my own book, but never got around to it. So finally on the evening of December 14, 2002, I started writing. I realized how hard it was to write a book. I had so many ideas that I did not know where to start. Somehow, just four weeks later I finished. I cannot believe it. Now, the long and arduous process of publishing is what I find ahead of me.

Like everything in life, there were numerous obstacles to get to where I am. I already have had three nasal operations. I have a hard time breathing and smelling. It is better now, but not 100%. Sometimes I can smell anything. Other times, I can't even smell garlic. I guess this obstacle really pushed me to write a book on something I love but cannot always fully appreciate.

HOW WINE IS MADE

THIS alone can be a thousand page book in itself. Winemaking is an extremely lengthy and arduous process. I can only speak of it in general terms. There are two places involved in winemaking: the vineyard and the winery.

In The Vineyard

Many wine makers always say, "Wine is made first and foremost in the vineyard." This is in a sense very true. If you have bad grapes, you are probably going to have bad wine. On the other hand, if you have good grapes, it will be easier to make good wine. There are many crucial components that determine everything in the vineyard. The main ones are:

Location
Weather
Vines
Grapes

Location

My father always told me how his father's wines always tasted different than his uncle's even though their vineyards touched. Differences in wine can be so varied even from grapes grown in neighboring vineyards. The ideal location for a vineyard is on a slope. Slopes get the most sunlight. It is as simple as that. Altitude is also important but varies greatly depending on which grapes are being grown. Riesling and Sauvignon Blanc do well at high altitudes while Zinfandel and Shiraz do well at lower altitudes (just as an example). Some vineyards are situated next to rivers, which are ideal because they act as heat storage places for grapes. Other vineyards, like those in Rhône have stones on top of the soil which also capture and trap heat. The soil must be well drained in order to provide the vines with an optimum supply of water and nutrients.

Weather

Each vineyard has its own climate, better known as microclimates. To be even more specific, each vine has its own microclimate. Each of these microclimates heavily influences the vines and therefore the grapes. Again, certain grapes do better in cool climates, while others prefer hotter climates.

Vines

Good vines make good wine, right? Pretty much, but it is not that easy. When vines are young (under 25 years) they produce a lot of grapes and in turn a lot of wine. This is a winemaker's gift from God. Plentiful crops help pay the bills plus pay for momma's brand new bag. As vines get older, (35 years+) they begin to produce less grapes, but of much higher quality. These vines are usually called "old vines" or in French "vielles vignes". Too many winemakers rip out older vines for the guaranteed cash crops. Younger vines produce more and that is usually the winery's goal. Though older vines produce better more expensive wines, "Old Vines" on a label does not always guarantee quality. Some wineries make bad wine from old vines and still charge too much money. Vines also have their share of hard times. They have to fight off various fungal and bacterial infections, including extreme weather temperatures. On top of that, they have to duke it out with every insect on the planet. A very important practice called Pruning helps maintain the vines to assure a high quality yielding crop. Pruning is when a wine maker clips away some fruit to keep the vines from over producing. This practice strengthens the vines and most importantly greatly improves the quality of the grapes. Pruning also makes harvesting a much easier process. Pruning will give you better grapes with concentrated flavors and less flaws.

Grapes

Picking the grapes at the right time is one of the trickiest things for a wine maker. They have to time it just right where the sugars and acidity are at their correct levels. Small, quick changes in weather can screw everything up. Harvesting may be done mechanically or by hand. The harvest is very decisive in determining what you will end up with.

In The Winery

Here is where man (or woman) can perfect or ruin everything.

General Steps to making Wine.

Red Wine

Red grapes are either completely or partially destemmed.

Then the red grapes are crushed.

The juice is left to ferment with the skins and sometimes even the stems.

The winemaker at this point may enact
Chaptalization or Acidification (only if the law of the country allows it).
Chaptalization is adding extra sugar if there is little in the must.
Acidification is the addition of extra acidity if there is little in the must.

The juice may be further kept in contact
with the skins and stems for extra color, flavor, and tannins.

The wine is then either transferred to
wood barrels (usually oak) or stainless steel vats for ageing.

The wine at this point may undergo a second fermentation
more commonly referred to as Malolactic Fermentation.
This converts the sharp tasting malic acid into lactic acid, which is softer.

All wines from all barrels or stainless steel vats are tasted and may be blended with other wines made from different grapes. White wine is sometimes blended into red.

The wine may or may not undergo a filtration process to remove unwanted impurities.

The wine is put in bottles and may remain at the winery for even further ageing which takes place in the bottle itself.

White Wine

White grapes are destemmed and then crushed.

The juice from white grapes rarely ever stays in contact with the skins.

The juice is fermented. At this point, Chaptalization or Acidification may be carried out.

The wine is then transferred to wood barrels or stainless steel vats.

The wine may undergo malolactic fermentation. This process is fine for red wines, but can make whites taste boring and milk like.

The wine may be blended with juice from other white grapes.

The wine is bottled.

Rosé Wine

Rosé wines can be made in 2 ways:

1) By fermenting the juice of red grapes with the skins for only a short period of time. Once the desired color is obtained, the skins are separated from the juice.

2) By blending white wine with red wine. This practice is illegal in Europe except in the French region of Champagne.

The wines may undergo malolactic fermentation.

The wines may be aged in oak barrels or stainless steel vats.

The wine is bottled.

Sweet Wine

Sweet wines can be made in 2 ways:

1)   By stopping the fermentation early. At this point, not all the sugar has been converted to alcohol. The remaining sugar is called residual sugar.

2)   The must is so high in sugar, that the fermentation may stop by itself leaving a lot of the sugar not converted to alcohol.

The sweet wine may be aged in oak barrels or stainless steel.

The wine is bottled.

NEW WORLD WINES

THE term New World wines refers to all the countries that are pretty new to the wine game. These New World countries (U.S.A., Chile, Argentina, New Zealand, Australia, and South Africa) borrowed the grapes from Europe and attempted to model their wines after those in France and Italy. The resulting wines are by no means similar to those from Europe. New World wine countries consistently follow trends without failure. Trends however do not necessarily coincide with quality. California is THE symbol and leading representative of the New World wine countries. I have tasted some amazing New World wines, most hailing from California. I have also tasted a lot of crap, mostly from California.

How did California wine get so popular? I do not know. The typical answer is that the California producers did this and that, experimented with cutting edge whatever, and a whole bunch of other boring stuff. In the U.S.A., California is known as "The Wine Country." What does that mean? Whole countries like France, Italy, and Spain are wine countries in their entirety. My answer: California wines achieved success because the "Wine Country" is a wine business not a wine producer. I have no problems with big business. In fact, I have no problem with California wine companies. I have a problem with the fact that people have to pay obscene prices for ordinary crap. Actually, let me replace the words "have to pay" with "willing to pay". That's right. The problem is the consumer. The big California wine companies will give the consumer what they want. My advice is to educate yourself as a consumer and then demand better. Ask and you will receive. Believe me, your dollars will not be denied.

California wine companies spend a ton of money on trying to get you to drink their wine. The wine shy consumer is so afraid of wine that they run to the name they have heard over and over again. They think they are playing it safe, but in reality they are playing it wrong. Chances are if you buy a California wine (white or red) you are getting something that is more of a concoction than wine. Phrases like "aged for a refined flavor" are misleading. Instead, wood chips and sometimes even powder essences are stirred in to add flavor. Sometimes this process is so overwhelmingly evident, it tastes as if they put wine in a bucket of wood chips.

California also unfortunately prides itself with making 100% of the wine strictly from one grape. They rarely blend. Blending can enhance certain positive characteristics or may soften the wine's rough character. It can even bulk up a boring wine. With California wines you are usually getting 100% Cabernet or Merlot (which is useless by itself) and many others too. The problem is you are getting all the Cabernet and Merlot that is available and that includes the *possible* negative aspects of those grapes. On top of that you are getting the exaggerated expressions of the grape. More is not necessarily better and California wine producers don't get that. To be fair, neither do Australia and Chile. Unfortunately, some Europeans are abandoning old, tried and proven styles to instead produce "New Style" wines. These people are shooting themselves in the foot and increasingly losing credibility among true wine lovers.

Consumers have started to get mad and now buy less and less. As with most New World wines, if you had one you had them all. Why drink the same crap every night? Also, why drink the same crap at such high prices? You might think, "Oh, why is this guy so extreme?" I am not and neither are the thousands of customers who are giving the California wine industry a deserved cold shoulder. I have my views. They are not extreme just because you might not happen to agree with them.

California is waking up. They have representatives go from store to store, restaurant to restaurant. I see them regularly. They have me blind taste some California wine and then ask me how much I think it is worth and how much would it actually sell for. My estimated worth was always at least half of the asking price. If I said a certain wine was worth $20, it sold for $45. I did not know whether to laugh or cry.

I would estimate that only 10% of all California wine is actually worth buying. Unfortunately, eight out of ten good to great California wines are quite expensive. There is great California wine out there, but it is quite rare. I do not mean to bash California wines. I JUST WANT TO PROTECT THE CONSUMER.

If you wish to discover New World wines, I suggest you direct your attention to New Zealand, specifically this country's whites. As a New World wine, it is still primarily fruit driven, however much better balanced and more food friendly than most others.

CRITICS

WHEN you point the finger at someone, there are three pointing back at you. People's ignorance of wine (and food) has allowed a host of jobs to pop up. You have magazines, TV shows, classes, you name it. People's fear of wine has given tremendous power to certain people, sometimes the wrong people. Some people are so scared of living, they would not even pass gas without first consulting a magazine. Big magazines have so many wine judges who are told not to give certain wines a bad score. Can you guess why? Well, think about it. If my winery gives your magazine $500,000 a year for advertising, would you have the guts to give my wine a bad score? Add to that a few hundred wineries and you have a rich magazine scared to tell the truth about so many wines. Then there are newsletters authored by an individual taster. This is somewhat fair. You can get to know the person's tastes by reading his/her opinions. Either you agree or you do not. The only problem is that some of these writers are so famous and powerful, that their word is believed to be law. Winemakers will change their whole style of wine making just to please the taster and receive high scores. These scores can really make or break a winemaker. Most tasters are very dedicated and love wine. They know so much about wine but still never get it. My point is that enthusiasm does not necessarily qualify you.

Do not get me wrong; there are some real good critics out there. The only problem is that these people are a minority and rarely noticed. In this book, I give countless descriptions of many different wines. I felt like an idiot writing the word "cherry" over and over again. The fact is most red wines do have hints of cherry. You can read all the descriptions you want about wine, but it will mean nothing until you try it. Who knows? You might know more than the critic. It does happen, by the way. The best story is when a journalist from a very important wine publication (no name) did not know that Sangiovese was an Italian grape. He actually thought it was Californian. These are some of the idiots in charge of judging people's hard work and to make matters worse they are getting paid. It is unbelievable.

TASTING WINE

I must begin first by saying that you should drink what you like. If you think it is good, then drink up. Apart from specific likes and dislikes, every one of us has a certain preference or tolerance for various degrees of richness, lightness, sweetness, bitterness, acidity, and tannins. Remember: One person's trash is another's treasure. There is no real correct way to judge what is good or bad; however there are certain steps one should follow when tasting wine.

You may start by pouring roughly 2 ounces into a wine glass of at least 12 ounce capacity. The extra space is crucial for swirling. Swirling is a process that opens up the wine's aroma and releases its flavors. Swirling may seem difficult, but practice will make perfect. For starters, first place the glass on a table holding it by the stem and rotate it in small circles. Once you get the hang of it, you can do it off the table while holding the glass in mid air. BE CAREFUL. I have seen many people attempt swirling and end up throwing the wine all over their own and the next person's shirt.

Wine tasting can be broken down simply into:

Appearance
Smell
Taste

APPEARANCE

A wine's appearance can be the first indicator of what you are about to taste.
Appearance can be further divided into 3 elements, which are:

Color Intensity, Color Hue, and Clarity

Color Intensity

The color intensity of a wine will indicate if a wine is full, medium or light bodied. For red wines, deeper color is *usually* better, but this is not necessarily true. Some Pinot Noir can be so light they are almost see-through.

Color Hue

Colors obviously vary for red and white wines. The various colors are:

White Wines:
<u>Pale green to yellow</u> Typical of younger wines especially those made from grapes grown in cooler climates.
<u>Straw color</u> The typical color of white wines recently released to the market.
<u>Yellow Gold</u> Typical color of older white wine and young sweet dessert wines.

Gold Typical color for older aged white wine and fuller bodied dessert wines.
Brown This color means that the white wine has gone bad. Only Sherry should have this color.

Red Wines:

Purple The color of very young wine.
Ruby Typical color of dry red wines and young Port wines.
Brick Red Indicates that the wine is maturing.
Red to Brown The stage at which dry red wines can start to turn bad; however definitely still drinkable.
Tawny The wine has gone bad. Only Tawny Port wines should have this color.
Amber Brown Another indicator that the wine has gone bad. Only Sherry wines should have this color.

Clarity

Wine should not have any cloudiness or haziness, which mean the wine is flawed.

SMELL

What you smell is what you get. Smell and taste are closely connected. After analyzing the appearance, you must swirl the wine in your glass. This allows the aromas to open up and then you start to smell. Put your nose inside the glass (not all the way) and inhale gently. You may smell hints of fruits such as oranges, lemon, pineapple, grapefruit, apple, peach, apricot, banana (plus hundreds of others) for white wines. For red wines, you may smell blackberries, cherries, cassis, tar, chocolate, prunes, licorice, tobacco plus a million more.

TASTE

Here we go, the last and most decisive step—tasting the wine. Smelling the wine can tell you a lot, but tasting will allow you to fully evaluate it. Take a small sip and swirl it around in your mouth. This swirling allows the tongue to take in all the wine's flavors. For bigger red wines, chewing the wine may be more appropriate than swirling it in your mouth. Sucking in a little air while the wine is in your mouth allows the aromas and tastes to come out more. Now swallow the wine and take notice to how it tastes and what impression it might leave you with.

You should judge the wine by:

Sweetness/Dryness
Acidity
Body
Tannins
Alcohol
Bitterness
Finish
Balance

SWEETNESS/DRYNESS

Red wines are almost always vinified completely dry. Some white wines made from grapes such as Rieslings, Gewurztraminer, and Chenin Blanc have just a slight touch of sweetness due to the residual sugar. Sweetness is detected at the tip of the tongue and must be balanced by high acidity. The more sugar a grape has, the more aroma and flavor. Pretty simple stuff, huh? Dessert wines are very sweet and have a good amount of residual sugar. Sometimes, over-oaked wines such as New World Chardonnays give off hints of sweetness. This sweetness appears as a vanilla like flavor imparted from the oak barrels.

ACIDITY

Very important component of wine. It is detected by its tartness and should be relatively high especially for white wines. The acidity is a wine's backbone. The higher the acidity, the longer the ageing capability. If the acidity is high, you get a wine with life that is food friendly. The acidity also acts as a preservative. Wines with high acidity are Riesling, Chianti, and Sauvignon Blanc (just to name a few of the many).

BODY

A wine's body is judged by its texture and weight in the mouth. This texture and weight is a combination of extract, alcohol, and acid. If the wine feels rich and heavy in the mouth then it is full bodied. A lighter, crispy, almost watery wine would be considered a light bodied wine. Medium bodied wines fall somewhere in the middle of the two. Dessert wines tend to be fuller bodied because the residual sugar adds weight and texture. That is why a grape such as Riesling is so amazing. Even if made into a dessert wine, Riesling has such high acidity that the wine feels light as a feather in the mouth. The acidity counters the grape's sugars.

TANNINS

Tannins are astringent substances most often found in red wines. The tannins usually come from the grapes' skins, seeds, and stems as well as the oak barrels in which they may be aged. Tannins appear rough in the mouth but soften if the wine is given time to age. Tannins as well as acidity give wines good structure. Wines that are tannic are Cabernet Sauvignon, Sagrantino, and Barolo (just to name a few).

ALCOHOL

Excess alcohol is easily noticed and is unfortunately all too common in New World wines. Excess alcohol gives your mouth a hot feeling. Alcoholic wines are the worst things to pair with any spicy foods.

BITTERNESS

The word bitterness is thrown around today like it's a Frisbee. Bordeaux wines are not bitter. They are earthy (a positive characteristic). True bitterness is a detriment and can be easily detected at the back of the mouth.

FINISH

The finish of a wine is the impression it leaves you with after it has been swallowed. If the wine's impression remains with you for quite a while, then it is called a long finish. If the wine's impression disappears after being swallowed, then the finish is short.

BALANCE

My favorite word. All of a wine's components must be judged from their relationship to each other. If none of the components overpower each other, then the wine is well balanced. Too many New World wines can be easily dissected. None of the flavors seem to integrate. It is almost as if there is a separation between each element. If a wine has a lot of fruit then it must have a lot of acidity to back it up. There must be a yin yang relationship to present a wine with pure harmony.

GENERAL WINE TERMS

ACIDITY: Acidity is noted in a wine by a tart feeling in the mouth. High acidity is a good thing regardless of what some people may say. It gives a wine life and it keeps things interesting. Excessive acidity is not necessarily great but it's better than flat tasting oak juice. The acidity brings out the flavors in a wine and the food you are eating. There are many kinds of acids, the main ones being: malic acid, tartaric acid, and lactic acid. Malic acid gives tastes of raw green apples. Tartaric acid has a more ripe citrus taste. Lactic acid is rounder and it dulls the wine. Lactic acid is like milk. Obviously, malic acid is the best, especially in white wines.

AERATION: To air out a wine, for red wines specifically. The aeration process opens up the wine and softens it. The aeration process can be exercised either by decanting or by swirling in a glass. European red wines, especially older ones, benefit highly from aeration.

AGEING: The process of ageing allows the wine to mature and develop flavors. It can round out the sharp edges. The tannins soften and occasionally shed to become sediment. Certain red wines must be aged. White wines, on the other hand, are not always meant to age. Of all white wines, Rieslings are the most age worthy thanks to its high level of acidity. It would be better if almost all white wines were aged in stainless steel tanks and not oak barrels. Ageing in oak barrels softens the wine much more than stainless steel. Oak barrels give off tannins and the trademark hints of vanilla. The toasty flavors in wine also come from the ageing in oak barrels. The smaller the oak barrel, the more of its flavor it imparts on the wine. Stainless steel lets the wine keep its freshness, making it not as soft as oak aged wine. The wine may be further aged in the bottle before its release to the market.

ALCOHOLIC: A term that describes a high alcohol wine that tastes hot in the mouth.

ANTHOCYANINS: The pigments found in the grape that give wine its red color.

APPASSIMENTO: A process in which the grapes are semi-dried, losing almost half of their water content. As a result, the sugars become concentrated and therefore the flavors are intensified. Passito refers to wines made by this process. This is the very same process that produces the world famous and exceptionally unique Amarone wines.

APPELLATION: A designated wine growing area that is governed by certain laws specific to each country.

France has **AOC** (Appellation D'Origine Controlée)
Italy has both **DOC** (Denominazione Di Origine Controllata) *and*
DOCG (Denominazione Di Origine Controllata e Garantita)
Spain has **DO** (Denominacio de Origen)
Portugal has **DOC** (Denominacao De Origem Controlada)
The United States has **AVA** (American Viticultural Area)

AROMA: What you smell in the glass. The term "bouquet" is sometimes used to describe the aroma in older, aged wine.

AROMATIC: No explanation needed for this one. At least I hope not.

BARREL: A wooden container that is used to store and age the wine. Oak is the most popular used wood for barrels.

BARRIQUE: A 225 liter oak barrel that is much smaller than older, more traditional oak barrels. The small size imparts more of the oak's flavors and components to the wine.

BIG: A term to describe a wine that is full bodied and rich. The flavors are concentrated and intense. New World wines tend to be bigger than big and therefore seem clumsy and without balance.

BITTER: Too many people confuse this term. A wine is bitter if it went bad. Some wines can have positive attributes such as bitter chocolate or bitter cherries. A wine novice would drink Bordeaux and deem it bitter. European wines tend to be earthy not bitter.

BLENDING: To combine different wines to create a certain flavor profile. This profile would not be possible had only one grape been used. The blend may use juice from different grape varieties, different years, different regions, different countries, or from different barrels. An example is blending Merlot to add softness to a big tannic Cabernet Sauvignon wine.

BODY: The feel of the wine in the mouth. The weight and texture is judged to see if the wine is full, medium, or light bodied. Light bodied wines can be perceived as watery and well, light. Full bodied wines are rich and heavy in the mouth. Medium bodied wines are somewhere in between. Many dessert wines are considered full bodied because of the residual sugar, which adds weight and texture.

BOTRYTIS CINEREA: A fungus that grows on the grape and can be of great benefit. Under the perfect circumstances, the fungus can cause the grape to boost its own sugar levels. In this case, Botrytis Cinerea is called noble rot and the wines are made into beautiful dessert wines. Gray rot, on the other hand, is bad and ruins the grape.

BOUQUET: The aroma of a wine, typically an aged and mature wine.

BREATHE: The wine breathes as soon as it is exposed to air. Decanting a wine into a decanter allows it to fully open. The wine softens and opens up. The initial funky taste and smell of some wines can actually wear off and expose good bold fruit. This aeration process is essential for most European red wines, especially older ones.

BRIGHT: A fresh fruitiness enhanced by a higher level of acidity.

BRUT: The driest category for Champagne.

BUTTERY: A term used to describe a buttery smell and taste in a wine, usually New World Chardonnay. Either oak ageing or malolactic fermentation may bring about this buttery hint (or both). Personally, buttery white wine makes me sick just typing it. White wine should be crisp, not buttery.

CASSIS: A term used to describe the taste and smell of black currants in a wine. Typical of Cabernet Sauvignon based wines.

CEDAR: A term used to describe a taste and smell of cedar wood in wine. Cigar Box is a synonym. Some red wines can possess this positive attribute. If a white wine has this hint, then it was aged in oak barrels and that's usually a no-no.

CHEWY: A term used to describe a dense and rich wine. These full bodied wines are almost always red (they *should* be). They are meaty enough to be considered chewy.

CLASSICO: The Italian word for classic. It is meant to describe an area within a wine region that usually has the oldest wine tradition and best wines.

CLEAN: Drink German Rieslings and you'll understand this term better.

CLOSED: A wine that does not expose its character. Time for ageing may be necessary for the wine to open up.

CORKED: A wine that went bad due to a faulty cork is referred to as corked. Up to 7% of all wines are unfortunately corked. If people eventually get over the useless tradition of cork, wineries will switch to screw caps and we can all enjoy good wine that never spoils.

CRAP: This is not an *official* wine term, but when you taste crappy wine, what else are you supposed to say? Synonymous with: Junk, S#*t, Is this a joke?, Gasoline, etc.

CRISP: A description for highly acidic wine. The acidity does wonders for wine, especially white wine.

DEEP: The intensity and depth of a wine.

DELICATE: Wines of great quality that are delicate, elegant, and refined.

DEMI-SEC: French word for "half dry".

DOUX: French word for "sweet".

DRY: A term to describe a wine that has had all its sugars converted to alcohol. Most beginners fear the word sweet and think dry is good. That is half true and half false. Most wines are dry. A wine novice who asks for a dry wine actually desires a sweet wine. They crave California Chardonnay, which are so oaked that they are sweet. The oak imparts a sweet vanilla flavor to the wine. These wines are made dry but taste sweet. So considering a California Chardonnay to be dry is *somewhat* contradictory.

EARTHY: A term to describe a wine that displays hints of earth and damp soil. This is considered a positive attribute in red wines.

ELEGANT: A term for wines that are delicate and exude finesse.

EUCALYPTUS: A term used to describe a mint-like aroma and taste in a red wine.

FERMENTATION: The natural process in which the yeasts (primarily found in the grape skins) convert the grape juice into wine. The yeasts help convert the grapes' sugars into alcohol and carbon dioxide. The carbon dioxide usually escapes via the air. In making Champagne, the carbon dioxide is trapped purposefully to create its characteristic effervescence.

FILTERING: A process in which the wine is filtered to improve clarification just before bottling. The filtering process removes yeast cells and other unwanted particles. It also removes sediment. Some winemakers believe that filtering may remove some flavor that the sediment offers to the wine. These producers label their wines "Unfiltered". It is typical to find deposits of sediments on the bottom of "Unfiltered" bottles or in your glass. Do not panic, it is harmless and it will not kill you. Fining is a similar process.

FINESSE: The trademark of German Rieslings. Finesse is a term used to describe a wine that is elegant, graceful and well balanced.

FINISH: A wine's finish is the impression it leaves in your mouth after it is swallowed. The taste and texture may linger and this is referred to as a long finish.

FIRM: This is self-explanatory. It describes a wine that has a good amount of tannins and a high level of acidity, but still well balanced.

FLABBY: Another self-explanatory term. The opposite of firm. Flabby wines lack the main source of life: acidity. These wines are usually oaked to add some interest, but I am not fooled easily.

FLAT: A synonym for Flabby.

FLESHY: A term used to describe a full bodied wine that is high in extract and alcohol. A synonym for Chewy, and the opposite of Lean.

FLINT: A positive characteristic of very dry white wines. It is a term that describes the smell and taste of flint striking steel. Typical of French wines such as Chablis and Sancerre.

FLORAL: Floral wines have aromas of flowers. Pretty simple, huh?

FORTIFIED WINE: A wine that has had extra alcohol or brandy (in most cases) added to boost the alcohol level up to at least 17%. Port, Madeira, Marsala, and Sherry are fortified wines.

FRESH: A wine that is alive, thanks to the acidity. It is used for clean and bright wines.

FRIZZANTE: The Italian word for "lightly sparkling". The next step in effervescence is Spumante.

FRUITY: Describes wine that are, well, fruity. The wine can exhibit hints of any fruit. You name it. Even cooked fruit. Fruitiness must be backed by acidity to be presented in a well balanced package.

GAMEY: A term to describe older red wines that display notes of game animals. It can seem borderline decayed and for some is an acquired taste.

GRAPEY: A term used for wines with reminiscent hints of raw grapes.

GRASSY: A term that describes the smell and taste of freshly cut grass. This is the most typical characteristic of Sauvignon Blanc wines.

GREEN: A term that holds many meanings. In one sense it might describe the grassy hints noted in white wine. It may also imply that a wine is not yet ready to drink and has a high acidic, under-ripe taste.

GRIP: A term that typically describes red wine that has a firm grip. This is a result of a high level of acidity and tannins.

HERBACEOUS: A term to describe wines with a smell and taste of herbs (fresh or dried). A typical description for white Sauvignon Blanc and Cabernet Franc wines. Herbal is a synonymous term.

HONEYED: A term used to describe the honey like fragrance and taste in a wine. Very typical of sweet Muscat wines and many other dessert wines.

INKY: The term which describes the "inky" deepness of some red wines.

JAMMY: A term to describe the concentrated fruity aroma and taste of a wine.

LEATHERY: A term to describe the leather smell occasionally found in some big tannic reds. The leather hints are usually extracted form the oak barrels during ageing.

LIVELY: A term that is used to describe a wine that is fresh. The high level of acidity is what terms a wine lively.

LUSH: A descriptor for wines that are rich but still soft and velvety.

MACERATION: The amount of time that the grape juice stays in contact with the grape skins, seeds, and sometimes stems. The goal is to extract components which would enhance the wine's texture, flavor, aroma and color. Maceration for red wines is usually longer than the ones for white wines. Stems, seeds, and skins can contribute unwanted elements to white wine.

MALOLACTIC FERMENTATION: Also called Secondary Fermentation. This process converts malic acid into lactic acid. Malic acid is the one that is responsible for a wine's juiciness and is the life of the party. Lactic acid is soft, round, and dull. Acceptable for red wines, but should be a no-no for all white wines. Almost every New World Chardonnay (specifically Californian) undergoes malolactic fermentation. The little acidity in these wines are further dulled (eliminated, if you will) and then sentenced to the oak chamber of death. Lactic acid makes white wines taste like milk. Go ahead! Have a cup of that with your meal and throw up!

MATURE: A term that describes a wine that has fully developed from ageing and is ready to drink.

MEATY: A synonym for Chewy.

MINTY: A synonym for Eucalyptus.

NOBLE: A term that describes a wine with noble character. Drink good Vino Nobile di Montepulciano and you will understand this term better.

NOBLE ROT: A synonym for the good strain of Botrytis Cinerea.

NOSE: A term that describes the wine's aroma or bouquet.

NUTTY: A descriptor for wines with a nutty characteristic. Good sign for Sherry, but a too common problem for California Chardonnays due to excessive oak flavoring.

OAK: Oak is the wood of choice for barrels used in ageing wine. The oak imparts flavors and even gives tannins. This is a good thing for red wines. For white wines, it spoils everything and turns the wine sweet with vanilla and toast tastes. It can be essential for certain reds, but can mask certain flaws in a white wine. Unfortunately, for some winemakers, the oak itself can be a flaw. Wines like these are termed oaked, which can be a positive or negative attribute (depending on the wine and your opinion).

OFF: A term that describes wine that has gone bad.

OFF DRY: A term for wine that has the slightest hint of sweetness,

OPEN: A wine that shows its offerings and is ready to drink. An open wine is the opposite of a closed wine. Older wines need time to open up. This is achieved by decanting.

OVERRIPE: A term for wine made from grapes that were left hanging way too long on the vine. The acidity is lost and the fruitiness is overbearing. It has sadly become a trend for New World wineries to make wine from overripe fruit. My advice: Save your money and buy a can of grape soda. It's the same thing but cheaper.

OXIDIZED: A term for wines that have been exposed to air for a long time. The air deteriorates the wine and renders it undrinkable. Oxidization is only a beneficial process for Sherry or Madeira wines. In these cases, the air gives the wines their characteristic nutty-caramel flavor.

POMACE: Pomace is what is left after the juice has been pressed from the grapes. The remaining elements are skins, seeds, and pulps. Sometimes the pomace is used to make Grappa or Eau de Vie.

POWERFUL: A term used to describe red wines that are full bodied, full flavored and have a high level of alcohol.

RAISINY: A term used to describe rich and intensely concentrated wines. The term is usually applied to dessert wines. Amarone is one of the very few dry table wines that are usually referred to as raisiny.

RESIDUAL SUGAR: The remaining sugar that is either purposefully or involuntarily left in a wine after fermentation.

RICH: A term that describes wines which are full flavored, full bodied, and high in alcohol. Robust is a synonym.

RIPE: A term for wines made from grapes that have fully developed its flavors. The ripeness of a grape is achieved by leaving the grapes on the vine for a little while longer. There is one problem. As the grape ripens, it boosts its sugar levels while the acidity level declines. A good winemaker should know when to pick the grapes so that both the sugars and acidity are in perfect balance. Very few grapes can pull this off. Riesling is such an incredible grape that it boasts high sugar levels as well as high acidity levels. It is like a genetic freak of nature given to us as a gift from up above.

ROSE: The French word for pink or rose colored. It refers to the wines of this color. White wines can be made from red grapes. When you squeeze a grape, the juice that comes out is clear, not colored. It is only when that pressed juice stays in contact with the grape skins, seeds and pulps (maceration) that the wines gain color. Rosé wines are made from red grapes but the pressed juice is left in contact with the skins for only a short period of time. The result is a pink wine with a little more body, fruit, interest, and of course color. Rosé wines should be served chilled.

ROUGH: A term for wines too tough to drink. The roughness can soften if the wine is allowed time to age.

ROUND: A term for well balanced, full bodied wines with no sharp edges.

SECOND LABEL: Second label wines are like a winery's runner up. The winery's second place nominee. The wines can usually be quite good and come at a lesser price.

SEDIMENT: The deposit at the bottom of the bottle or wine glass. Typically found in older red wines. When a wine ages, it loses some of its tannins and softens up. Those shed tannins form the deposit known as sediment. Do not be alarmed. Sediment is harmless. It is very typically found in Port wine. Sediment can and should be easily removed. When decanting a wine, be careful to do it slowly, so that the sediment does not pour over from the bottle into the decanter.

SMOKY: A term for wines that display smoky aromas or tastes. This smokiness may be inherent in the soil, which bears the vines or may come from excessive ageing of the wine in oak barrels.

SPICY: A self-explanatory term for wines that have aromas or tastes of spices such as: cloves, cinnamon, nutmeg, or pepper. The red grape Shiraz and the white grape Gewurztraminer are typically described as spicy.

SPUMANTE: The Italian word for sparkling. Spumante wines have more bubbles than Frizzante wines.

STEELY: A term that describes a white wine's lean body and high acidity. Usually a good attribute.

STRUCTURE: Another self-explanatory term. It includes a wine's acidity, alcohol, fruit, body, tannins, etc. All wines have structure, it is just a question of it being well structured or not.

SWEET: The term sweet is usually applied to taste. Sweetness is detected on the tip of the tongue. Sweetness comes from the residual sugar left after fermentation. Sugar must be balanced by acidity (something not common). Some grapes are intrinsically sweet and this sweetness is further exhibited in the wine. Sweetness can also come from ageing in oak barrels.

SYRUPY: A term that can be used to describe thick, sweet wines.

TANNINS: Tannins are astringent substances found in the grape skins, seeds, stems and even the oak barrels in which they are aged. They give red wine flavor, texture, and structure. Tannins can also behave like antioxidants and allow the wines to age gracefully. With age, the tannins turn from rough to soft and are occasionally shed. These shed tannins form a deposit at the bottom of the bottle called sediment. Wines with noticeable tannins are referred to as tannic. Tannins feel dry and puckery in the mouth and the back of the throat.

TAR: A descriptor for wines that smell of tar. Barolos typically display hints of tar.

TART: A wine that is high in acid. Crisp is a synonym.

TERROIR: The famous French term which literally means soil. Terroir is used to describe wine and is not only limited to soil. Terroir embodies everything. That is, every and anything that might influence the taste of the wine. Terroir includes the grapes, the soil, the amount of sun, the angle of the vineyard to the sun, the water drainage, the altitude, etc.

TEXTURE: Yet another self-explanatory term.

THICK: A self-explanatory term. Thick wines are dense and rich.

TOASTY: A term for wine with aromas and tastes of toasted bread. Toast hints come from ageing in oak barrels and are all too common for Californian Chardonnay.

TOBACCO: A term to describe the aroma of tobacco in some red wines such as Spanish Rioja.

UNFILTERED: Wine that has not been filtered. Unfiltered wines typically have sediment at the bottom of the bottle.

UNDERRIPE: A term for wine made with grapes that were picked not yet ripe. Such wines have high acidity and very little sugar levels.

VANILLA: A term for wines with vanilla like aromas. This aroma is derived from ageing in oak barrels. Very common in New World wines. Sometimes it is all you taste.

VARIETAL: A wine that uses the name of the main grape from which it is made. Very common practice for New World wines.

VEGETAL: A term that describes wines with aromas and tastes of vegetables such as bell peppers. This is typical of wines such as Cabernet Franc. Even Cabernet Sauvignon can be vegetal if the grapes are grown in cooler areas.

VINTAGE: A term that describes the year of the grape harvest and the wine made from those grapes. The word vintage wine is not intended to denote quality. Only in Port and Champagne does the word vintage specify quality.

WATERY: A very light bodied wine.

SERVING AND STORING WINE

Red wines are best served between 56 – 60 degrees Fahrenheit.

White wines are best served between 45 – 50 Fahrenheit.

Rosé wines are best served between 45 – 50 Fahrenheit.

Good Champagne should never be served too cold. Optimum serving temperatures for good Champagne is between 48 – 52 Fahrenheit. Champagnes of lesser quality should be served colder.

Sweet Dessert wines are best served between 45 – 50 degrees Fahrenheit.

Fortified wines are best served between 55 – 60 degrees Fahrenheit.

Cognacs, Armagnacs, and other Brandies are best served between 55- 60 degrees Fahrenheit.

Grappa is best served between 45 –50 degrees Fahrenheit.

Wine should be stored in a cool dark place. Wine hates heat, light and vibration.

Storing **LEFTOVER** wine is always confusing to most people. The best thing to do is pour the remaining wine in smaller wine bottles, known as half bottles or splits. This will minimize the amount of air in contact with the wine. The next thing to do is get something called a vacuum wine saver. This gadget takes out roughly 60% of the remaining air. If the wine is white, put it back in the fridge. For red wine, store it in a cool place.

THE WINE COUNTRIES

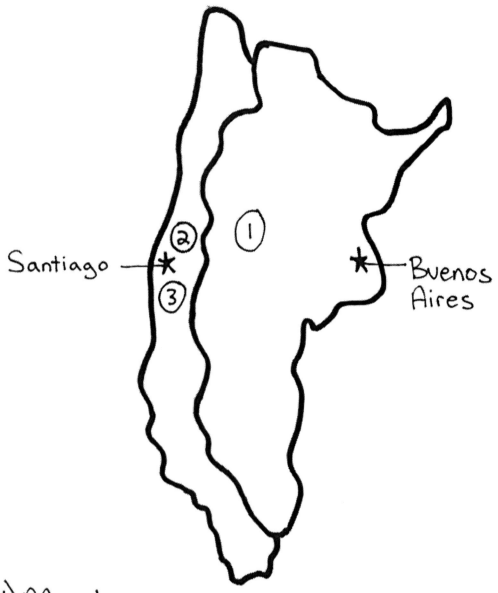

Santiago

Buenos
Aires

1) Mendoza
2) Maipo
3) Colchagua

CHILE and ARGENTINA

ARGENTINA

ARGENTINA is one of the few places in South America that produces wine. Argentina and Chile have many residents of European lineages (particularly Spanish and Italian). These European immigrants have brought with them their love and need for wine. Argentina produces a lot of wine but it is usually nothing great. New producers are coming in and attempting to change that. The country does well with international varieties. This is a good thing because they have no choice but to import foreign grapes. Argentina has no indigenous grape of any significant importance.

Mendoza is the main growing region.

Mendoza plants mostly Malbec and Cabernet Sauvignon. The two French grapes are more fruit driven than they are when made in their birthplace. The Malbec in particular is made more accessible. Malbec wines are known as "black" and some deem it undrinkable, but Mendoza Malbecs are a little easier. The perfect match for Malbec is beef (Argentina's number one food).

CHILE

THIS country burst onto the wine scene in the last decade. They were greeted with tremendous enthusiasm and appreciated for their outstanding value. Low prices kept Chile and many consumers smiling, but after a while people started sobering up. They asked themselves, "How much Cabernet and Merlot can I drink?" They also started to realize that although buying good Chilean wine could be a fun and inexpensive experience, it could be quite repetitive and boring. Many foreign investors from France, the U.S., and even Spain rushed to Chile to plant vineyards by the mile. Chilean wine can be good and satisfying, but remember they are New World wines and the aim is immediate gratification. The wines are usually huge with a lot of fruit.

Chile has two main wine areas:

Maipo Valley
Colchagua

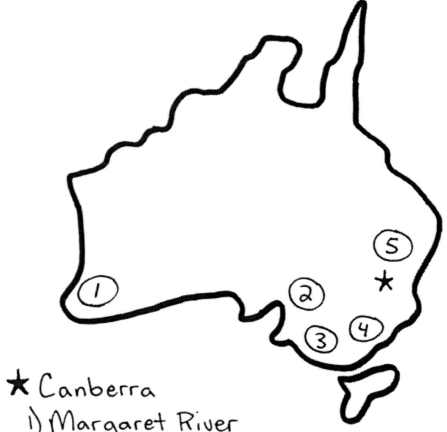

★ Canberra
1) Margaret River
2) Barossa Valley
3) Coonawarra
4) Yarra Valley
5) Hunter Valley

AUSTRALIA

AUSTRALIA

AUSTRALIA has had vineyards for a very long time, but quality wine is a relatively new phenomenon. Australia has no indigenous grapes of any importance. They rely on the trustworthy and obviously very marketable international varieties. One variety in particular, Shiraz, does very well. Shiraz is the Australian term for the French grape Syrah. Australia also plants large amounts of Cabernet Sauvignon, Merlot, and Chardonnay. There are other varieties planted as well but none do as well as the above mentioned. Australia is huge but most of its vineyards (and the best ones) are located in the South East. Australian wines are considered New World. The style is big, oaky, fruity, and alcoholic. Too many Australian wines (along with Californian) are ridiculously monstrous and do not match well with too many foods. As with other New World wine, if you had one wine…you had them all. If I go into detail about a whole category of wines which are almost all pretty much the same, I would be wasting your time and mine.

SOUTHWEST	SOUTHEAST
Margaret River	Hunter Valley
	Yarra Valley
	Coonawarra
	Barossa Valley

SOUTHWEST

MARGARET RIVER

Relatively new wine zone producing Cabernet Sauvignon, Merlot, Shiraz, Chardonnay etc. Not much to talk about. Try some and then move on with your life.

SOUTHEAST

HUNTER VALLEY

This is where you get GOOD Australian wine. World famous for the Shiraz produced in this area. Semillon and Chardonnay are very popular white grapes here. The Shiraz from Hunter Valley is best served with red meat.

YARRA VALLEY

Best known for its red wines like Pinot Noir and Cabernet Sauvignon. The Pinot Noir goes best with poultry and other light white meats while the Cabernet stands up well to red meat.

COONAWARRA

Famous area that produces primarily Cabernet Sauvignon and Shiraz for reds and Chardonnay for white.

BAROSSA VALLEY

The Barossa Valley makes a lot of Riesling wine, none of which compares to the incredible German stuff. The reds are Grenache and Shiraz blends that most resemble fruit driven versions of a French Côtes du Rhône.

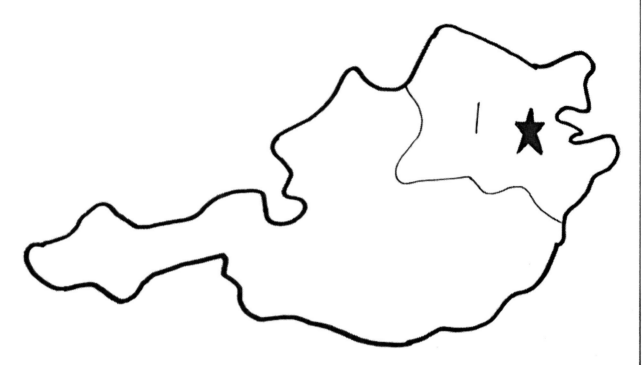

* Vienna
1) Niederosterreich

AUSTRIA

AUSTRIA

AUSTRIA is one of the last places a wine novice thinks about when buying wine, or even discussing it for that matter. Why? I ask. The same goes for Germany. Enter the mind of a wine fanatic and you will discover Austria usually occupies a seat on his/her Top 5 list (especially and specifically for white wine). The wines of Austria can be very similar to those of Germany. They both plant similar grapes like Riesling and Gewurztraminer. The weather in Austria is cool but a little hotter than Germany. This Austrian climate produces Rieslings and Gewurztraminers that are bigger, drier, more full bodied and with a higher level of alcohol than those of Germany. The native grape Gruner Veltliner is a wine lover's gift from God. This gift however usually does not come cheap. It is unfortunate that Austrian wine is very hard to find outside of Austria. To make it worse, people don't give Austrian wine a chance. To make it even worse, retailers and restaurants usually do not know anything about Austrian wines. Go ahead. Go into a wine store and ask for Austrian wines. They will look at you confused. Most don't even know Austria made wine. Most don't even know where Austria is! Most will confuse Austria with Australia and point you to a shelf full of overoaked Shiraz. My point is even if you were interested in Austrian wine (which you should be) you probably won't find any. I have decided to make my chapter on Austrian wine short and brief, because what's the point anyway?

Most of the Austrian wines are white and are made
in the eastern part in a region called Niederosterreich.

NIEDEROSTERREICH

Riesling
Gewurztraminer
Gruner Veltliner

RIESLING
The Rieslings of Austria are bigger, drier, and have a higher level of alcohol than the German ones. Hints of peaches are also present and as always these Rieslings are incredibly food friendly. Great with pork and cabbage dishes.

GEWURZTRAMINER
Another typical grape from Germany makes its way over here and does well. As is the case with Austrian Rieslings, the Gewurztraminers here are bigger, drier, and also have a higher level of alcohol. Great with spicy foods.

GRUNER VELTLINER
Gruner Veltliner is Austria's pride and joy. The grape is kind of like Riesling but totally different (if you know what I mean). Gruner typically displays hints of peach, white pepper and even is herbaceous with hints of celery. This wine is high in acidity and leaves your mouth feeling clean and refreshed. Perfect with fish and shellfish. Great with green vegetables as well as poultry and other white meats.

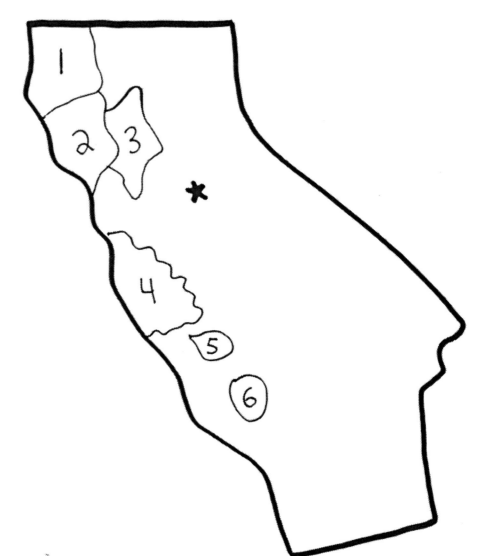

★ Sacramento
1) Mendocino
2) Sonoma
3) Napa
4) Monterey
5) Paso Robles
6) Edna Valley

CALIFORNIA

CALIFORNIA

    CALIFORNIA has entered the wine market and took it by storm. As impressive as this whirlwind of new style wines may be, do not forget that storms will always leave damage behind. California wine can be really great just as it can be utterly disgusting. Quality unfortunately does not come cheap. Audacious prices are charged for quite ordinary stuff. Variety would never be the right word to describe California's wines. All the wines are made from famous international varieties such as: Cabernet Sauvignon, Merlot, Pinot Noir, Shiraz, Chardonnay, Sauvignon Blanc, etc. Zinfandel is a widely planted grape that was once thought to be native to California, but has later been discovered to be a descendant of Italy's Primitivo grape. The grape varieties are few and to make matters worse, most California wines are remarkably similar. They also demonstrate the typical "bigger the better" American standard applied to most things crafted in this country. This standard is what makes them too big for most foods. The grapes are too ripe and eventually too oaked. There is usually a lack of balance in California wines.

    There are some amazing wines I have tried from California. These typically come at high prices. If you really want to challenge yourself, find a *good* $10 bottle of California red or white that tastes *unique*. I am willing to bet you would return empty handed. California wineries are waking up and are promising to implement changes. They realize the potential California has to produce great wine. They are attempting to devise a way to offer these wines at lower prices.

    California wines are too big, too fruity, too alcoholic, and too much of everything else. These wines are meant for immediate gratification. This would also explain why California wines do not and cannot demand auctioning powers like the Bordeaux wines of France. The Bordeaux wines can age forever and are considered investments. Wasted potential is very sad. California can soar to the top if they just take advantage of what they have.

California boasts many wine regions.
The main ones to know are broken down geographically.

NORTH	**CENTRAL**
Mendocino County	Monterey County
Sonoma Valley	Edna Valley
Napa Valley	Paso Robles

NORTH

MENDOCINO COUNTY

Mendocino County has many wine areas but the one to know is Anderson Valley. Anderson Valley is cooler than most California's wine areas and does well with Chardonnay. The acidity is higher and the grapes do not become over ripe like most others in the state. Many reds are also made but the focus seems to be on the white Chardonnay grape.

SONOMA VALLEY

Sonoma has quite a few wine areas but the main ones to know are:

Alexander Valley
Dry Creek Valley
Russian River Valley
Sonoma Valley
Carneros

ALEXANDER VALLEY
This area can produce great Cabernet and Chardonnay grapes. Many producers from around California buy their grapes from Alexander Valley. The region can be quite hot so Cabernets and Chardonnays are picked pretty ripe. The region also does well with many other grapes such as Zinfandel and Merlot.

DRY CREEK VALLEY
Dry Creek is hotter in the North so it can produce good Zinfandel, while the South's cool weather produces good Chardonnay grapes.

RUSSIAN RIVER VALLEY
This wine region is quite cool and can produce some great Chardonnay. French owned companies also produce some sparkling wine here.

SONOMA VALLEY
Does very well with Cabernet and Zinfandel. Mostly warm weather except in the South.

CARNEROS VALLEY
The southern portion of the Sonoma Valley is quite cool and can produce some good Chardonnay.

NAPA VALLEY

THE most famous wine region in the United States. The northern part has cooler weather than the southern portion. Wherever you go in this region, you will realize that Napa *is* Cabernet Sauvignon. It is wildly popular here and can produce the best in the whole state. The best of Napa can rival even the best in the world. Some of the most expensive wines of America come out of Napa Valley.

CENTRAL
MONTEREY COUNTY

Chardonnay reigns supreme in this cool weathered wine region. Riesling is also very popular although the best examples are equal to average German Rieslings.

EDNA VALLEY

The cool weather is ideal for great Chardonnay, if it is not excessively bathed in oak barrels. Also makes some of California's better Pinot Noir.

PASO ROBLES

A hot region that primarily produces Cabernet and of course Zinfandel. The wines tend to be very alcoholic.

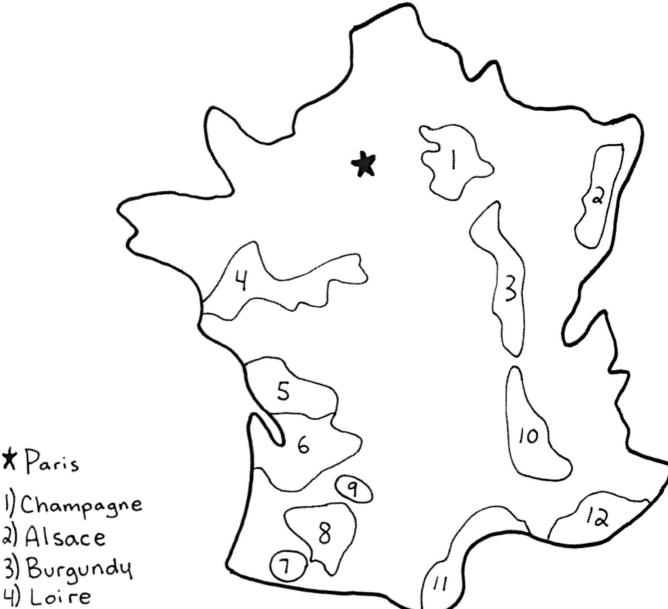

★ Paris

1) Champagne
2) Alsace
3) Burgundy
4) Loire
5) Cognac
6) Bordeaux
7) Madiran
8) Armagnac
9) Cahors
10) Rhône
11) Languedoc Roussillon
12) Provence

FRANCE

FRANCE

FRANCE has long been the standard bearer in the wine world. Almost all of the famed international varieties hail originally from France. Here, however, the grapes do not taste as they do in the New World. The grapes offer earthier hints and are less fruity. French wines are meant to go with French food. With a lengthy history and proud traditions under its belt, France has played the role model through out much of wine's history. France has perfected the art of living or *joie de vivre*. The French winegrowers should be considered breeders. They simply took wine to the next level.

The French are credited with inventing numerous terms, terroir being one of the very important. The literal meaning of terroir is soil, but it is meant to imply much more. Terroir implies everything. The water, the grapes, the slopes, the weather, the angle to the sun, the cultivation, the soil, etc, etc.

The Romans brought their viticulture to France. Since then, the love affair the French have with wine has developed into one of the country's many cultural foundations. This love affair marched forward and produced throughout history the most elaborate classification of wines, specifically in the region called Bordeaux. The French have over time figured out which grapes grow perfectly in the right place. They have stuck with these guidelines and have obviously reaped the rewards and gained maximum success.

This success has unfortunately inflated certain people's egos and led the greedy to charge astronomical prices for wine even during bad years. Some of the most prestigious wineries have (in bad years) turned out wine that is not worth a third of their already ridiculously high asking price.

With all that said, I urge people to learn about French wines and their well-organized system of wine classification. Many (almost all to be exact) French wines should be consumed with food.

NORTHWEST: LOIRE

NORTHEAST: CHAMPAGNE
ALSACE

CENTRAL WEST: BORDEAUX
COGNAC

CENTRAL EAST: BURGUNDY

SOUTHWEST: CAHORS
MADIRAN
ARMAGNAC

SOUTHEAST: RHONE
PROVENCE
LANGUEDOC-ROUSSILLON

Many French wine regions are further divided into districts or subdivisions. The wines may be named after the town, or district, or (very rarely) by grape. The regions listed above, all have subdivisions and districts. Listed below will be only the major ones. Including all of them would be long and quite boring.

NORTHWEST

LOIRE

Pouilly Fumé
Sancerre
Vouvray
Muscadet
Anjou
Chinon

Pouilly Fumé
The word fumé in French means smoke. It is meant to describe the character of the wine made by the white Sauvignon Blanc grape. The Sauvignon Blanc here is crisp and acidic with grassy and herbaceous tones. Good Pouilly Fumé is getting pricier by the year. Do not confuse this with Pouilly Fuissé wines, which is a totally different wine made from the white grape called Chardonnay.

Sancerre
Sancerre is world famous for its white wine made from Sauvignon Blanc. Strikingly similar to the whites of nearby Pouilly Fumé, Sancerre is actually considered to be THE place for Sauvignon Blanc. Red wine made from Pinot Noir is also produced, but is not as good as the Sancerre whites. The most important part of wine enjoyment is matching it with the food of the very same region where it is made. The Loire Valley is famous for its goat cheeses. Sauvignon Blanc wines and goat cheese are the absolute perfect marriage of food and wine. Try it and I guarantee you will agree.

Vouvray
Made from the great white grape called Chenin Blanc. Very unique tastes of green apples and boasts high acidity. Chenin Blanc is noted for its welcomed slight sweetness. Very minerally, Vouvray is excellent with shellfish and fried seafood. Also a beautiful match with pork and chicken. Can be made into sweet dessert wines and even into sparkling wine.

Muscadet
This white grape is also known as Melon de Bourgogne. These wines can be fairly average. The best are Muscadet de Sevre-et-Maine. Even better, look for these wines with the words *mise en bouteille sur lie* written on the label. These wines have nice hints of lemon and orange. They are generally softer with a slightly creamier mouth-feel. Great with shellfish.

Anjou
Famous for its rosé wines. There are two kinds of rosés made here: Rosé D'Anjou and Cabernet D'Anjou. Rosé D'Anjou is made primarily from Malbec and Gamay. Cabernet D'Anjou is made from Cabernet Franc and Cabernet Sauvignon.

Chinon
THE red of the Loire Valley. Made primarily from the Cabernet Franc grape. Chinon wines are typically lighter but some examples are able to age for up to 10 years. Chinon has high acidity, raspberry and black currant hints. It is best known for its herbal, bell pepper taste.

NORTHEAST

CHAMPAGNE

Only sparkling wine from this region may legally be called Champagne. Located about one and a half hours (90 miles) northeast of Paris. The weather of Champagne is cool and unsuitable for many grapes except ones like Chardonnay, Pinot Meunier, and Pinot Noir (among a few others). The cool weather prevents the grapes from fully ripening and developing a high level of sugar. The acidity, however, is kept at a high level. The low sugar/ high acidity balance is exactly what is needed for good Champagne. Champagne has approximately 49 million bubbles per glass. The more bubbles create a textured and creamy feel in the mouth. The bubbles are THE most important part of Champagne. The high acidity should allow your mouth to feel clean and refreshed after a sip of Champagne. Good Champagne should *never* be served too cold.

Vintage Champagne implies that the wine is made from
the best grapes of a harvest from a specific year.

Non Vintage Champagne is a blend of wines from at least 2 separate years.
Non Vintage Champagne is made the same every year.
The type of Champagne you get will be almost exactly the same from year to year.
Three of every four bottles of Champagne produced are Non Vintage.

Rosé Champagnes are made by adding a small amount of red wine to the blend or by leaving the red grape skins in the must during pressing to give off color, body and fruit.
Rosé Champagnes are generally better, although it is a matter of taste.
These wines also cost more.

On the label, you will see either: Brut, Extra Dry, Demi-Sec, or Doux.
These terms describe the level of sweetness (Brut being bone dry while Doux is sweet).
Champagne is one of the best choices for appetizers, fish, shellfish, and fried foods. Its high level of acidity gives Champagne the privilege of being very food friendly. NEVER serve Champagne in those flat saucer-like glasses. The flatness quickly eliminates the bubbles (the sole purpose of Champagne). You must always use tall flute shaped glasses. Also, never serve Champagne in either a chilled or wet glass. It will lessen the top's desired "foam".

ALSACE

Whites	**Sparkling**
Riesling	Cremant D'Alsace
Gewurztraminer	
Pinot Gris	
Pinot Blanc	

Whites

Riesling

The best white grape finds a comfortable home here in Alsace (the French eastern region that borders Germany). These French Rieslings are typically the driest of all. They also are the most full bodied and highest in alcohol. These Rieslings should be reserved for heavier fare, while the Germans match better with lighter fare. Great with any pork, chicken or duck dish.

Gewurztraminer

Originally from Italy, this white grape is gaining popularity. The word "gewurz" is German for spicy and that is exactly what kind of wine this grape can produce. Gewurztraminer is fuller in body than Rieslings and is very floral with dense hints of peach. Great with any heavier pork, chicken, or duck dish.

Pinot Gris

Completely different style of wine than the Pinot Grigio of Northern Italy. Here in Alsace, Pinot Gris is rich, fat, and honeyed. Luscious hints of pear and apple are supported and balanced by high acidity and a minerally touch. Great with foie gras.

This grape may also be called Tokay D'Alsace. Not to be confused with Italy's Tocai Friulano or Hungary's Tokaji Aszù.

Pinot Blanc

Not as creamy and spicy like Pinot Gris. More subtle hints of apple and spice. High acidity makes this a very food friendly wine.

Sparkling

Cremant D'Alsace

A great non-Champagne alternative. Made from Pinot Gris, Pinot Blanc, Riesling, and Pinot Noir. These dry sparklers are great with shellfish, fish and many different appetizers. Hard to find, but definitely worth the search.

CENTRAL WEST

BORDEAUX

Bordeaux is broken up into 5 main districts:

Pomerol	Médoc	Sauternes
Saint Emilion	Graves	

Médoc is further divided into: Margaux
Pauillac
Saint Estèphe
Saint Julien

POMEROL

Pomerol is the smallest of the five main districts. Its wines are made primarily with the red grape called Merlot. Small amounts of Cabernet Sauvignon and Cabernet Franc are added; however these two grapes are usually softer and less tannic than in other parts of Bordeaux. Pomerol wines are pretty big and rich considering it is made from Merlot (a grape known mostly for its softness). Good Pomerols usually exhibit hints of earth, blackberries, dark chocolate, nuts and licorice. Good Pomerols are also expensive. Great with lamb dishes. Pomerol whites (along with other Bordeaux whites in general) are never really significant.

SAINT EMILION

Saint Emilion is considered to be the second best of Bordeaux (first being Médoc). Made primarily from Merlot grapes. Occasionally blended with Cabernet Franc and Cabernet Sauvignon. Typically softer and easier drinking than other Bordeaux wines. They are less tannic and higher in alcohol. Unlike New World Merlot based wines, Saint Emilion wines can mirror Pomerol, with its earthiness and softness. Also ideal with lamb dishes. Its whites are never really significant.

Médoc

Médoc is broken up into 4 main areas:

Margaux
Pauillac
Saint Estèphe
Saint Julien

Margaux
One of the best in the Bordeaux region. Margaux wines are made primarily from Cabernet Sauvignon grapes. Cabernet Franc, Merlot, and Petit Verdot are also blended in the wine. These are some of the legendary Bordeaux wines that can age for a very long time. Margaux wines are known to be very elegant with an incredibly balanced and perfumed bouquet. These Cabernet based wines differ from New World Cabernets in the sense that they hold back on overemphasizing the fruit. Margaux wines tend to be earthier and are much better suited for meals than 90% of New World wines. Great with red meats and many other artery clogging foods.

Pauillac
The biggest and roughest of the Bordeaux wines, Pauillacs are meant to age very long. Huge body with very firm structure. Made from Cabernet Sauvignon grapes and may be blended with smaller amounts of Cabernet Franc, Merlot, Malbec, and Petit Verdot. These wines can be beasts, so pair it with some serious fare.

Saint Estèphe
The most tannic and age worthy wine of Bordeaux. Typically not as good as the other Bordeaux wines. Primarily made from Cabernet Sauvignon with smaller amounts of Merlot, Cabernet Franc and Petit Verdot. Today, producers are using more Merlot to help soften these austere wines. The average ones are quite pricey and good ones are even pricier.

Saint Julien
The smallest communes in Médoc. Cabernet Sauvignon is the dominant grape with Cabernet Franc, Merlot and Petit Verdot used in small amounts. Some believe Saint Julien wines to be some of the best in the world. Sometimes, they are right. Saint Julien is also very pricey. Age worthy and very elegant. Great with red meat.

GRAVES

Graves are made primarily from Cabernet Sauvignon grapes. Smaller amounts of Merlot and Cabernet Franc are blended. Graves reds can be very similar to those in Médoc. Graves, however, are typically softer than Médoc wines due to the higher percentage of Merlot. Graves wines are great ageing wines and have that characteristic earthiness so prevalent in Bordeaux wines. A great choice for grilled meats.

SAUTERNES

THE dessert wine of France. Known worldwide, Sauternes demand high prices. Semillon (white) is the main grape; however tiny amounts of Sauvignon Blanc and Muscadelle may be added. Good Sauternes have golden hints of almonds, honey, peach apricots, pineapple and even coconut all presented as a creamy, rich and textured masterpiece. Great accompaniment to blue cheeses or foie gras.

COGNAC

The town Cognac is world renown for producing the famous brandy with the same name. Brandy is essentially liquor that is distilled from wine and then aged in wood. Brandy may be made using other fruits. An example is Calvados (made from apples). Since this is a book about wines made from grapes, then Cognac will be discussed and Calvados will not. Cognac is made primarily from the white Trebbiano grape (in France called Ugni Blanc). After fermentation, the wine is distilled twice. It is then placed in Limousin wood casks to age and mellow its sharp and harsh taste.

Stars on the label imply that the wine has been aged.
The more stars, the more ageing, and therefore the higher the quality.

You will see these terms on the **older** Cognac bottle's label:
V.S. (Very Superior)
V.S.O.P. (Very Superior Old Pale)
V.V.S.O.P. (Very, Very Superior Old Pale)

The label terms: X.O., Extra, and Reserve usually mean
that the Cognac is the oldest one put out by the producer.

The label term Fine Champagne means that at least 60% of the grapes
come from the better vineyards of Cognac called Grande Champagne.
If it says Grande Fine Champagne, all the grapes come from that area.
DO NOT CONFUSE this with Champagne (the northeast region which produces sparkling wine).

CENTRAL EAST

BURGUNDY

Burgundy has 5 main regions:

Chablis
Côte D'Or
Côte Chalonnaise
Maconnais
Beaujolais

CHABLIS

Chablis makes white wine using the Chardonnay grape. Chablis is considered (by the smart people) to be Burgundy's best white. Oaked little if any, Chablis whites are very high in acidity and boast its characteristic lemony notes. They have a flinty and mineral quality. The cool climate prevents the grapes from ripening too much, so the acidity stays high. This allows Chablis to be perfectly food friendly. Great with shellfish, fish, and white meats.

COTE D'OR

Côte D'Or is divided into 2 parts: **Côte de Nuits** and **Côte de Beaune**

Both produce fabulous red and white wines; however
Côte de Nuits is famous for its red wines while Côte de Beaune is famous for its whites.

Côte de Nuits
World famous for its Pinot Noir. Considered to be possibly the best Pinot Noir wine in the world. Côte de Nuits has numerous villages, which are famous for their wines and even carry the villages' name on the label. The better known villages are Vosne-Romanée, Gevrey-Chambertin, Nuits Saint-George, and Vougeout (among others). The medium bodied reds from here are high in acidity with spicy cherry notes. Here, Pinot Noir offers hints of earthiness. Great with hams and creamier cheeses such as Brie.

Côte de Beaune
World Famous for its Chardonnay. Considered to be the best Chardonnay wine in the world. Côte de Beaune also has numerous villages that are famous for their wines and even carry the villages' name on the label. The better known ones are Meursault, Chassagne-Montrachet, Puligny-Montrachet, Savigny-Lès-Beaune, Aloxe Corton, and Auxey-Duresses (among others). These Chardonnay based wines are typically medium bodied. In Meursault, the wines are nuttier and butterier. In Montrachet, the wines can be more concentrated and smoky. Côte de Beaune whites can be and usually are the most expensive whites in the world. Pommard and Volnay are basically the two villages that produce the best Pinot Noir in the Côte de Beaune. Pommard can even be quite full bodied (considering it is made from Pinot Noir).

COTE CHALONNAISE

Côte Chalonnaise produces both red from Pinot Noir and white from Chardonnay. Not considered as good as other Burgundy whites. New producers are creating better wines, but as a whole, these wines are nothing to go crazy for.

MACONNAIS

The Maconnais is well known for its white wine made form Chardonnay. It is typically lighter bodied and fermented in stainless steel tanks. Maconnais whites are crisp and minerally. Cheaper and actually better than Côte Chalonnaise. Should be drunk as early as possible. Pouilly Fuissé is the most famous appellation and produces some of the better whites of the Maconnais.

BEAUJOLAIS

The most southern part of the Burgundy region. It differs from the rest of Burgundy because it makes wine made from the red grape Gamay. These wines are known to have hints of raspberries, cherries and black pepper. It has very little tannins and little alcohol but its acidity level is pretty good. All Beaujolais wines should be drunk young. Beaujolais Nouveau should be drunk immediately after production. Beaujolais Nouveau (new in French) is wine made toward the end of every year. The Gamay grapes are pressed and bottled immediately. It is a fresh young wine that is released every third week of November and should be drunk until January.

SOUTHWEST

CAHORS

This area produces what will forever be referred to as "black wines". This is because the wines produced primarily from Malbec grapes are very dark, tannic and need time to age. Malbec is usually used for blending in Bordeaux, but here it is a shining star. It exhibits dark flavors of raisins and tobacco. Makes a great accompaniment to steak. It is like the Guinness of wine (an acquired taste). So hurry up and acquire!

MADIRAN

If Cahors is an acquired taste, then I do not know what to say about Madiran. Tannat is the dominant grape. It is red and produces very big, dark, tannic and rough wines. So big and rough in fact, that big grapes like Cabernet are used to soften Tannat up. These wines need time to age and even then should only be paired with red meat.

ARMAGNAC

Armagnac is a region that makes very fine brandy under the same name. Armagnac is considered one of the world's best brandies, second only to Cognac. Armagnac is distilled only once whereas Cognac is distilled twice. If brandy is distilled less, it is left with more pronounced flavors. Armagnac is also aged in wood. The wood, called Black Oak, gives more flavor than Cognac's Limousin Oak. The Black Oak also speeds up the ageing process. Usually fuller than Cognac, Armagnac lack's Cognac's finesse.

SOUTHEAST

RHÔNE

The Rhône region has many growing areas.
The main ones to know are:

Côtes du Rhône
Côte-Rôtie
Condrieu
Hermitage
Crozes- Hermitage
Cornas
Gigondas
Châteauneuf-du-Pape
Tavel

Côtes du Rhône
This is the general term applied to red, white, and rosé wines produced in the Rhône region. These wines are typically inexpensive and blend Syrah, Grenache, Cinsault, and Mourvèdre for the reds, while using Marsanne, Roussanne, and Grenache Blanc grapes for the whites. The whites are never anything extraordinary. The reds can be very good and prices are never too high. Red Côtes du Rhône can be light bodied, medium, or even full bodied. Either one, these wines will always have spicy and peppery hints with soft red and black fruits. These characteristics come from the Syrah and Mourvèdre grapes. Meant to be drunk earlier than other Rhône wines. Good with chicken dishes, lamb dishes and even pizza.

Côte-Rôtie
The most northern part of the Rhône region. Côte-Rôtie produces only red wines made from Syrah and a maximum of 20% of white Viognier grapes. The Syrah lends the spiciness and peppery traits, while the white Viognier offers the big exotic aromas.
Côte-Rôtie has notes of blackberries, raspberries, and cassis with a hint of smokiness. One of the more elegant of the Rhône wines. These rich and full bodied wines can be some of the best in the world. Côte-Rôtie can and should age for quite a while. Beautifully paired with grilled meats especially those with heavier sauces on them.

Condrieu
Condrieu makes only white wine made from the Viognier grape. Viognier is very aromatic. It has strong notes of apricots, peaches, honey, and spice. Acidity, unfortunately, can be quite low. Very little is produced, so it is hard to find and pretty expensive. Great with spicy cuisines and a natural pair with pork and chicken.

Hermitage
Hermitage is well known for its reds and whites, but the reds are what leave people dreaming. Made primarily form Syrah with occasional blends of a little white Marsanne and Roussanne grapes. Hermitage wines are very big, robust, and powerful. They are meant to age. These wines are tannic and full bodied with notes of tar. Not as elegant as Côte-Rôtie. Amazing stuff and obviously expensive. Great with heavy fare. Again, RED meat.

Crozes- Hermitage
These wines are very similar to Hermitage, although usually not as good. Softer and less intense than Hermitage. Good but not worth it when you can get Hermitage for either the same price or maybe a little more.

Cornas

Increasingly becoming more popular, Cornas makes only red wines primarily from the Syrah grape. The wines can be some of the biggest and most tannic in all of Rhône. Although hard to find, Cornas is worth it. Many believe Cornas will only get better and soon wine drinkers everywhere will direct their attention to this place.

Gigondas

Made primarily from Grenache grapes. Sometimes blended with Syrah, Cinsault, and Mourvèdre. Big wines with high levels of alcohol. Gigondas has dark fruits and benefits from a few years of ageing.

Châteauneuf-du-Pape

Either THE best or at least tied with Côte-Rôtie for the number one spot in Rhône. Châteauneuf-du-Pape makes very little white. The reds are so good that nobody ever cares about the whites. The dominant red grape is Grenache. It is usually blended with smaller amounts of Syrah, Cinsault, and Mourvèdre (among others). Châteauneuf-du-Papes are easily recognizable by the imprinted papal coat of arms logo on the bottle. These wines are huge and earthy with full flavors of raspberries, black berries, black currants and herbs. Good Châteauneuf-du-Pape can be expensive but if any wine is worth the extra cash, it is THIS. Excellent with red meats.

Tavel

This area makes only rosé wine. These rosés are fuller and drier. Made primarily from Grenache and Cinsault. Considered one of the world's best rosé wines.

PROVENCE

There are 2 main areas:

Bandol
Coteaux d'Aix en Provence

Bandol

Better known for its red wines made from Mourvèdre. Good rosés are made from Grenache, Syrah, and Cinsault. Up and coming wine area that represents good value in an oversaturated expensive marketplace. Definitely worth the search.

Coteaux d'Aix en Provence

Mostly noted for its reds and rosés made from Cabernet Sauvignon, Cinsault, Grenache, Syrah, and Mourvèdre. Also represents an incredible value among too many overpriced and over-marketed French wines. Find some.

LANGUEDOC-ROUSSILLON

There are many wine areas.
The ones you should know are:

Corbières
Faugères
Fitou
Minervois
Saint-Chinian

Corbières
Produces wine primarily from Carignan. Nothing really special. High in alcohol and tannins and quite spicy.

Faugères
These reds are good to very good on average. They are made primarily from Rhône varieties such as Grenache, Syrah, Carignan, Cinsault and Mourvèdre. Getting better year-by-year and is worth a try.

Fitou
Possibly the best of this region. Made from Carignan, Cinsault, Grenache, Syrah, and Mourvèdre. Great with the famous bean dishes of this area.

Minervois
Full bodied red made with Carignan and Grenache. Getting better every year especially with larger additions of Syrah and Mourvèdre.

Saint-Chinian
Along with Faugères and Fitou, Saint-Chinian takes its place as one of the best southern French reds. Saint-Chinian uses Carignan and Grenache with steadily increasing percentages of Syrah and Mourvèdre. Spicy and slightly herbal, these wines can be a little hard to find.

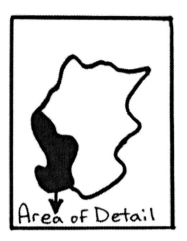

Area of Detail

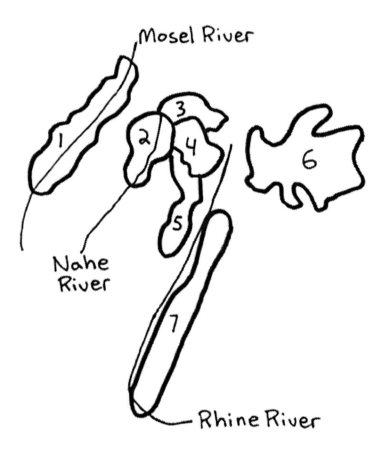

Mosel River

Nahe River

Rhine River

1) Mosel-Saar-Ruwer
2) Nahe
3) Rheingau
4) Rheinhessen
5) Rheinpfalz
6) Franken
7) Baden

GERMANY

GERMANY

WHAT is it that people do not get about German wines? Excuse me, what is it about *most* people? Germany unfortunately is typically overlooked and ignored in wine conversations. That is, in conversations with wine novices. Before I continue, I must acknowledge a man who has helped shape the minds of many wine lovers. This man is considered by many a radical, crazy, a nut job, etc, etc. I heard it all. But you know what? He is about 99% accurate on his opinion and understanding of wine. His name is Willie Gluckstern. He is a wine author, a wine teacher, and of course a wine importer. He is what the wine world has been waiting for. Throughout the book I took careful attention not to mention a producer's name or even certain brands. With this one; however, I feel it is a duty to talk.

Willie Gluckstern helped me along with countless others see the wonderful world of German wines. He more importantly helped unravel the lies, myths, and misunderstandings of so many of today's popular New World, New Style wines. His book is called "The Wine Avenger." If anything, I propose you buy his book over mine. I also highly suggest you enroll in his wine classes. Even better, I strongly suggest you discover his wines. Do these three things and I guarantee you will be better off.

Ok, back to business. Germany has been blessed with the capability to claim the number one spot for both the white grape Riesling and the wines it produces. Nowhere in the world can this grape prosper as well as in Germany. Nowhere in the world is there white wine so unique and *SO* good! I allow people to have their own opinions. BUT LISTEN UP! Riesling *is* the world's best white wine grape. Like it or not. If you don't agree, it is because you do not get it. Say anything about anything, but please hear me out on this one.

Riesling is genetically superior to almost any grape out there (FACT). People often mistake Rieslings as sweet wines. Oaked California Chardonnays are sweet wines. The oak gives off a vanilla creamy sweetness. Those Chardonnays are sweet.

Rieslings, on the other hand, have a very high level of sugar. I compare the Riesling grape to very good fruit, like a banana that is naturally high in sugars. The sugars in Riesling are perfectly balanced by its high level of acidity. Almost always, the sugar/acidity situation is a give and take. If you increase one, you will lose the other. This is not so with Riesling. It incredibly has high levels of both. More sugars mean more flavor and more acidity means it is more food friendly (FACT). Rieslings can be paired with more different foods than any other grape, white or red (FACT).

Thank God not too many people realize this because you can get great Rieslings for relatively cheap. On top of all this, Rieslings from Germany are low in alcohol, which makes it automatically more versatile. It is also possibly the grape that best expresses its terroir. Rieslings are so great that blending another grape in its wines could actually ruin it. It can stand all alone and be as pretty as it wants. In fact, Rieslings are blended in other boring wines to liven them up. In Alsace (France) and in Austria, the Rieslings are bigger, earthier and drier. In Germany they are lighter and have the least alcohol. German Rieslings are the most elegant whites around.

Germany's cool weather climate and soil types are perfect for making great white wine. The best vineyards are along the Mosel and Rhine rivers. The grapes are planted on slopes so steep (a good thing) that harvesting is usually done manually rather than mechanically. Other grapes that do well in Germany are Gewurztraminer, Muller Thurgau, Sylvaner, and Scheurebe. It is believed that these grapes play a lesser role in representing Germany's best wines.

VERY IMPORTANT!!!

When buying German Rieslings, you should take notice of certain words on the label. The German labels are very informative. Written on the labels are descriptions of ripeness. These words will tell you the <u>level</u> of ripeness. It tells when the grapes were picked and therefore the sweetness, acidity, and body of the wine.

The levels of ripeness are:

<u>Kabinett</u>: Dry, light to medium body, elegant, highest acidity with moderate sweetness.

<u>Spatlese</u>: The grapes are picked later so the grapes have a higher level of sugar. They are fuller bodied and fruitier.

<u>Auslese</u>: Very ripe. Medium bodied and a much higher level of sugar than the previous two.

<u>Beerenauslese</u>: Picked form a selected bunch of very ripened grapes (almost shriveled). Sweet enough to be considered dessert wines.

<u>Trockenbeerenauslese</u>: Picked even later. The grapes are very sweet.

<u>Eiswein (Ice Wine)</u>: As the name implies, the grapes are picked frozen. Most of the grapes' content is solid with very little liquid (of which is extremely concentrated). The grapes hang and are not picked usually until January. The sweetest of all. Only grapes like Riesling can produce such sweet wines and make them feel light in the mouth. The lightness comes from the grape's high acidity. This balance of sugar and acidity is unparalleled in any other grape.

Please Note:

Kabinett and Spatlese Rieslings may sometimes be divided into 2 categories:

Trocken: means dry, almost no residual sugar.
Halbtrocken: means half dry. Still pretty dry, but a little more body and fruit.

Germany has many wine regions.
The major 7 all lie along or between the rivers Mosel and Rhine.
These regions are:

Mosel
Nahe
Rheinhessen
Rheingau
Rheinpfalz
Franken
Baden

MOSEL

Mosel wines come in long, skinny *green* bottles. They are the wines with the lowest alcohol (7.5 – 10%) in Germany. The Mosel makes great Rieslings that are very delicate and elegant. These flowery wines display hints of the typical fruits of the fall season. Soft hints of apples, citrus, pears, and of course slate (from the soil the vines grow in). Great with so many foods, the list would be endless. Try it with light fish or shellfish.

The Mosel river has 2 tributaries: Saar and Ruwer.
These two both produce great Rieslings.

The Saar Rieslings come from a higher altitude and
have higher acidity and therefore can age longer.

The Ruwer Rieslings are the more delicate, elegant and smooth of the two.

NAHE

The Nahe is a river that actually lies in between the Mosel and the Rhine. The Riesling wines take on traits of both surrounding wine regions. The wines are very minerally, stony, and very aromatic. It has the elegance of Mosel wines with the heavier body of the Rhine wines. Nahe wines are great if you can find them. Perfect accompaniment to many fish dishes, shellfish, as well as appetizers and snacks.

RHINE

Rheinhessen, Rheingau, and Rheinpfalz are all wine regions associated
with the Rhine river. All three have similarities that define Rhine wines.

Rhine wines come in long, skinny *brown* bottles. They have a slightly higher level of alcohol (9 – 10%). The Rhine makes mostly Rieslings that are a little heavier in body, although still quite light and very elegant. These wines typically exhibit hints of summer fruits such as peaches, apricots, currants, and berries. Again, great with many different foods.

RHEINHESSEN

This wine region is located Northwest of the Rhine. It produces mostly Rieslings, which are softer than those from neighboring areas. These wines typically have smoky hints, with notes of roasted summer fruits. These wines are a steal. Some of the best value wines in Germany, and the world for that matter. This region is also a big producer of white wines made from Sylvaner. These wines are soft, light, and earthy with pretty good acidity. Can even display nice hints of smokiness and grapefruit. This region also makes wine from the white grape Scheurebe. This is a cross between Rieslings and Sylvaner and displays characteristics of both.

RHEINGAU

This region lies Northeast of the Rhine. It produces mostly Rieslings and is best known specifically for its Kabinetts. The Rieslings here are bigger and drier than most of the other German ones. They are richer and more full bodied with long ageing capabilities. Many top wine estates can be found here in Rheingau.

RHEINPFALZ (PFALZ)

This is Germany's warmest and driest wine region. Produces less Riesling wines than other German wine regions. The warm weather produces Rieslings that are full bodied, richer, and with a higher level of alcohol. Rheinpfalz is better known for its Gewurztraminer wines. Gewurztraminer is derived form the German word "gewurz" which means spicy. Typically, these wines are spicy with hints of flowers, in particular rose petals. They are fuller bodied than Rieslings. Here in Germany, Gewurztraminers are lighter than the ones from nearby Alsace and Austria. The German Gewurztraminer is fruitier, lighter, and lower in alcohol, with good acidity and medium sweetness.

FRANKEN

The cold weather of Franken is better suited for grapes such as Muller Thurgau and Sylvaner. Sylvaners from Franken are considered some of the best in the country. They typically display the earthiness so prevalent in all Franken wines. Sylvaner here is at its biggest and richest. They are also some of Germany's driest wines. Sugar levels are pretty low.

BADEN

The southernmost wine region in Germany. Known specifically for its Pinot Noir, known as Spatburgunder in Germany. The acidity is typically not as high as compared to other wines from neighboring regions. The Pinot Noirs can be so elegant, with bright cherry and strawberry fruit. Unbelievably food friendly, but also very hard to find.

*Athens
1) Macedonia
2) Attica
3) Peloponnese
4) Santorini
5) Samos
6) Cyprus

GREECE

GREECE

WINE has long played an important role in Greek life. Myths and stories describe the wines of Ancient Greece to have been quite good. Today's modern Greek wines unfortunately do not uphold this belief. For a long time, Greek producers have made less than mediocre wine and the Greek consumer kept his/her mouth shut. No one complained, so no improvements were made. There's some good news coming. People are starting to wake up. Producers are eliminating old techniques, which have proven ineffective. They now have adopted a newer approach, but always keeping it rustic and traditional. As usual, international varieties are also big here but the wines made from the indigenous grapes are the ones that are gaining interest. When the wines are made correctly, they can be good at pretty affordable prices. As always, Greek wine goes best with Greek food.

There are many wine regions in Greece.
The main ones to know are:

Peloponnese
Attica
Cyprus
Macedonia
Santorini
Samos

PELOPONNESE

The 3 main areas of Peloponnese to know are:

Nemea
Patras
Mantinia

NEMEA

Some of the best red wine of Greece comes from this area. The dominant red grape is Agiorgitiko (St. George). This grape can produce big, spicy wines with hints of plums and dark fruits. It has pretty low acidity, unless it is grown at higher altitudes. Also makes some pretty good rosé wine. Great wine for lamb dishes.

PATRAS

Mavrodaphne
A red grape that produces good dessert wine. The best come from in and around a town named Patras. This wine is full bodied and very aromatic. Ageing in oak barrels softens the wine. Mavrodaphne should be served at room temperature, not cold.

Muscat
The Muscat wines are sweet and aromatic. Big apricot scents. Peloponnese produces most of the better Muscats in Greece.

MANTINIA

Moscophilero
A good white Greek grape. It is typically added to wines to give character. It is considered to have both characteristics of Gewurztraminer and Muscat. It actually might have even higher acidity than both. It can be made as a white or even rosé.

ATTICA

Whites	Rosé
Retsina	Roditis
Savatiano	
Roditis	

Retsina
Retsina is made all over Greece, but in Attica they are particularly popular. Retsina can be any wine that has been flavored with pine resin. It is considered an acquired taste to non-Greeks. The usual grapes used to make Retsina are Savatiano, Roditis, and Assyrtiko. Hard to find outside of Greece.

Savatiano
The most planted grape in Greece is never anything special. It is typically used to make Retsina wine. On its own, it is average with low acidity and slight hints of oranges.

Roditis
Can be quite average. The better pink skinned varieties are usually added to increase quality and add complexity. Good acidity and should be drunk young. Enjoy with shellfish.

CYPRUS

Dessert

Commandaria

Commandaria

Made from the red grape Mavro, Commandaria can resemble Spanish Sherries. Good Commandaria is hard to find, but definitely worth it.

MACEDONIA

Reds

Xynomavro

Xynomavro

A very dark colored red grape that produces full bodied wines. It is very high in acidity and tannins. These wines are rich and spicy. One of the top reds of Greece. They are capable of ageing quite a while and are best suited for heavy fare. For now, the best wines of this region come from an area called Naoussa.

SANTORINI

Whites	Dessert
Santorini	Vino Santo

Whites

Santorini

The dry white wines of this region are labeled Santorini. Made from the white grape named Assyrtiko. If not oaked, these wines can be some of the best of Greece. It has high acidity and is stony and minerally. A food friendly wine that is perfect with fish and shellfish.

Dessert

Vino Santo

Greece's version of Italian Vin Santo. The Assyrtiko grape is used and the hot weather boosts the sugar levels. As a result, alcohol is usually quite high (15%). The grapes are dried in the hot sun, pressed and the wine is then aged. The result is a Oloroso like Sherry.

SAMOS

After Dinner	Dessert
Metaxa (Brandy)	Muscat

After Dinner

Metaxa

Greece's most famous brandy. Made primarily from the neutral white grape Savatiano. Muscat is usually blended to add sweetness and life to the brandy. The brandy is aged in oak for more developed flavors and aromas.

Dessert

Muscat

If made well, Samos Muscats can be some of the best values in the category of dessert wines. There is a big demand for these wines from this island. They typically have hints of apricots, peaches, and even citrus. Look hard for these wines, because they can be good for little money.

★ Rome
1) Valle D'Aosta
2) Piemonte
3) Liguria
4) Lombardia
5) Trentino Alto Adige
6) Veneto
7) Friuli
8) Emilia Romagna
9) Toscana
10) Umbria
11) Marche
12) Lazio
13) Abruzzo
14) Molise
15) Campania
16) Puglia
17) Basilicata
18) Calabria
19) Sicilia
20) Sardegna

ITALY

ITALY

OK, first of all let me start by saying that there is no way to have a complete book detailing Italian wines without it being tens of thousands of pages. There is so much to talk about; it is absolutely frustrating and sometimes quite discouraging. Clones included, there are over 2,000 different grapes in Italy, most of them with origins native to the land. As overwhelming as that may seem, look at it like this: You now have 2,000 reasons to experience Italian wine.

Before embarking on your journey through Italian wine, you must know that it is the largest producer of wine in the world and most of that wine is never and probably will never be exported. If you don't live in New York, Los Angeles or any other major city, your contact with the diversity of Italy's wines will be even less.

Like everything else in Italy, wine is something that is rooted deep in the land's history. It was made thousands of years ago and the Romans helped spread and plant vineyards across the world. They introduced new techniques and approaches to winemaking. There is now evidence that the Romans were actually the first to invent the type of wine we know now as Champagne.

Over these thousands of years, Italian foods and wines have seemed to form a perfect marriage that is unrivaled anywhere in the world. I believe Italian wine goes best with Italian food, while French wine with French food and Spanish wine with Spanish food, etc, etc. With Italian food and wine, however, the combination is woven together almost as if there was divine intervention. Go to Italy and eat REAL Italian food and you will see what I mean.

Italy is geographically one of the most diverse places on earth. From the Alps to the Mediterranean, its different landscapes offer totally different backgrounds for wines, food, and obviously people. The wines, food, people, art, architecture, scenery, etc, are all completely different from region to region, but are somehow harmoniously tied together under one nationalistic Italian feel.

What you eat and drink in the north of Italy, you probably won't even see in the south. Even the language is spoken differently from region to region. The Italian language has more dialects than any other in the world. It is probably the European language that changed the least since Medieval times.

The history behind Italy shines through every product made there. The wines express the nobility, tradition and feel of the very region they come from. With so many grape varieties, it is almost impossible to get bored of Italian wines.

The Regions

Italy has 20 regions, each with their own grapes and different styles of wines. All regions have the international varieties like Cabernet, Merlot, Chardonnay and so on. But who cares about those grapes when you have 2,000 new ones to meet and discover?

The wines are broken up by region.
All wines will not be listed, as it would lead to an unbearably long list to read.
Listed are just a few highlights from the 20 regions of Italy.

NORTHWEST:

Piemonte
Liguria
Valle D'Aosta

NORTH:

Lombardia
Emilia Romagna
Toscana

NORTHEAST:

Fruili Venezia Giulia
Veneto
Trentino Alto-Adige

CENTRAL:

Marche
Lazio
Umbria
Abruzzo
Molise

SOUTH:

Campania
Basilicata
Calabria
Puglia

The Islands:

Sicily
Sardegna

NORTHWEST

PIEMONTE

Whites

Gavi
Arneis
Moscato D'Asti
Asti Spumante

Reds

Dolcetto
Barbera
Barolo
Barbaresco
Nebbiolo D'Alba

Whites

Gavi
Made from the Cortese grape, this wine boasts very high acidity. It is quite delicate with hints of lime, but it is not quite aromatic. Great with fish and seafood. Not a wine to go crazy for but definitely better with more foods than overpriced oak juice from California.

Arneis
In Piemontese dialect Arneis means difficult; referring to the difficulty in growing and handling the grape. This wine has beautiful hints of apples, pears, grapefruit, licorice and nuts. Very versatile and accompanies fish well along with white meats and vegetables. Great with pesto sauces. It is usually from Roero DOC; hence you will see it sometimes as Roero Arneis.

Moscato D'Asti / Asti Spumante
Both wines are very similar and are made with a grape called Moscato Bianco. Half way through the fermentation, the wine is put in sealed tanks and the bubbles are trapped. This leaves a good amount of the natural grape sweetness

untouched. Moscato D'Asti is referred to as *frizzante* while Asti Spumante is just that: *spumante*. Asti Spumante has more aromatics with higher alcohol and is bubblier. Moscato D'Asti is fruitier with less alcohol and is less bubbly. These wines will always have soft and elegant hints of peaches and apricots. Absolutely perfect as an after dinner drink, but just as great for an aperitif. Matches very well with fried foods and shellfish. Though I disagree with pairing sweet wines and dessert together, Moscato D'Asti is one of the very few sweet wines I would pair with a sweet dessert.

Reds

Dolcetto
The name of this grape means "little sweet one". Oddly enough, Dolcetto really isn't sweet. Common flavors of Dolcetto are cherries. The flavors start ripe and fruity in the beginning and end dry while offering hints of bitter cherry on the finish. Licorice and even coffee can be found. It has low acidity so it can be drunk young. Dolcetto is the earliest ripening of the 3 main reds of Piemonte. It goes well with pizza.

Barbera
Barbera is very adaptable and easy to grow; making it one of the most planted grapes in Italy. It is medium bodied with low tannins and high acidity. Cherry flavors are dominant and if aged in oak it will develop tannins (something it is usually low in) and a plummy flavor. This makes a nice pasta wine.
The 3 main Barberas are:

> Barbera d'Alba: *Heaviest and most concentrated*
> Barbera d'Asti: *Medium*
> Barbera del Monferrato: *Lightest and most acidic*

Barolo
Made form 100% Nebbiolo grapes, this is the king of Italian wines. Tar and roses are the main scents of anything made from Nebbiolo. Full bodied and very complex with high acidity and is tannic as well. Leather, dried herbs (as well as fresh herbs), licorice, and dried cherries along with many other red fruits. Barolos are very earthy. Austere in their youth, Barolos get better with age. Modern Barolos are made to be drunk earlier. Drink Barolos with heavier, more serious food. Pair the wine with the local food of Piemonte such as beef, lamb, and pasta with truffles.

Barbaresco
Made also with Nebbiolo and strikingly similar to Barolo. Barbaresco, however tends to be a little lighter, fruitier, less tannic; therefore a little more easy drinking.

Nebbiolo D'Alba
THE grape of Piemonte. It is very late ripening. Harvest time is usually in November, a time when fog (nebbia) comes and surrounds the vineyards; therefore giving the name Nebbiolo. Same description as Barolo and Barbaresco but Nebbiolo D'Alba is lighter and fruitier than the first two. Great with Bresaola.

LIGURIA

Whites	Reds	Dessert
Pigato	Ormeasco	Sciacchetrà
Vermentino	Rossese	
	Sangiovese	

Whites

Pigato
A white grape with herbal hints and sharp acidity. It is floral, peachy and nutty. Very similar to Vermentino, but a little lighter with higher acidity. Great with fish and absolutely perfect with Pesto (this region's pride and joy).

Vermentino
Popular in Liguria, Sardegna, and even coastal Tuscany. In Liguria, it tastes more herbal than usual. As stated above, Vermentino is strikingly similar to Pigato but a little fuller and fruitier. Popular accompaniment to fish.

Reds

Ormeasco
This grape is actually Dolcetto under a different name. Very much the same as Dolcetto but a little lighter with earthier hints and more pronounced forest fruits such as red and black berries. Nice with pizza and light pastas. Also good with white meats.

Rossese
From the Dolceacqua DOC, it is sometimes known simply as Dolceacqua. Dolceacqua means sweet water. They are light, perfumy and have moderate acidity. Beaujolais–like in character, it is best served as an accompaniment to light fare.

Sangiovese
One of the most planted grapes in Italy (possibly THE most planted), it makes its appearance in Liguria as an earthier version of the Tuscan Sangiovese based wines. More earthy hints of mushrooms are prevalent. Great with pasta and beans.

Dessert

Sciacchetrà
The famed dessert wine of this area is nearly impossible to get. Very limited quantities are ever made. Using Bosco, Albarola, and Vermentino grapes, Sciacchetrà dessert wines are one of those rare sweet treats that come once every third blue moon.

VALLE D'AOSTA

Whites	Reds
Petite Arvine	Nebbiolo

Whites

Petite Arvine
White grape with high acidity. Also made as sweet or semi sweet wine. Very hard to find.

Reds

Nebbiolo
Here the Piemontese grape is lighter and fruitier with a higher level of acidity.

NORTH

LOMBARDIA

Whites	Sparkling	Reds
Riesling	Franciacorta	Valtellina
		Oltrepò Pavese

Whites

Riesling

The best white grape makes an appearance in northern Italy but in the Oltrepò Pavese area it produces one of the top in Italy. The high altitude and mountain cool climate help produce a lighter style Riesling that finishes crisp and dry like Rieslings from the nearby Friuli region.

Sparkling

Franciacorta

A DOC in the north. One can call this Italy's response to Champagne, but in reality Champagne is France's answer to Italian sparkling wine. It is now known that the Romans enjoyed sparkling wines way back then. Although typically French grapes (Chardonnay, Pinot Noir, Pinot Meunier) are used, the quality of good Franciacorta comes at usually half the price of the French sparkling wines.

Reds

Valtellina

The best Nebbiolo in Lombardia comes from this area. It is locally called Chiavennasca.
Nebbiolo here is at its lightest and most elegant. They also make a Nebbiolo passito, where the grapes are dried before pressing. This process concentrates the sugars and intensifies the flavors in the grape. It mirrors the process for Amarone in the neighboring Veneto region.

Oltrepò Pavese

The name breaks down like this: Oltrepò (over the Pò river) and Pavese (in the province of Pavia). This area produces very good Pinot Noir. Its cool climate is perfect for this delicate and hard to handle grape.

EMILIA ROMAGNA

Reds

Lambrusco
Gutturnio
Sangiovese di Romagna

Lambrusco

At its best when produced in Sorbara. Lambrusco can be semisweet or dry. It is slightly effervescent and is meant to be drunk young. Great with chestnuts and rosy hams. Also great with Parmigiano Reggiano.

Gutturnio
A blend of Barbera and Bonarda that may be vinified dry, sweet, or even into a frizzante. Cherries and chocolate are typical notes.

Sangiovese di Romagna
The Sangiovese wines here have less acidity and tannins than those from nearby Chianti. Still displays the typical red fruits like raspberries and cherries.

TOSCANA

Whites	Reds	Dessert
Vernaccia di San Gimignano	Chianti	Vin Santo
	Brunello di Montalcino	
	Rosso di Montalcino	
	Vino Nobile di Montepulciano	
	Super Tuscan	

Whites

Vernaccia di San Gimignano
The very first to receive DOC status in Italy, this famed wine comes from the even more famous town of San Gimignano. High acidity and nice citrus notes. Nice with shrimp and Tuscan beans.

Reds

Chianti
Everyone knows this one. Ranging from mediocre to excellent, Chianti is made always with a dominant percentage of Sangiovese. Blended in are other grapes like Canaiolo, Colorino, Trebbiano, and Malvasia. Very dry and boasts very high acidity, Chianti is popular for its cherry and raspberry characteristics. It typically can offer hints of tea on the finish. A stunning match with pasta and tomato sauce.

Brunello di Montalcino
Incredible when made correctly. Brunello is a larger version of the Sangiovese grape. It actually harvests quite early so it usually avoids October rains. Very big, full bodied with high acidity and a lot of tannins. Can age very long thanks to its well balanced structure. Essentially, a bigger, better and more refined version of Chianti.

Rosso di Montalcino
This is basically a junior Brunello. It is not aged as long. It is fruitier, slightly lighter and usually half the price. Rosso di Montalcino is a steal.

Vino Nobile di Montepulciano
The name literally means noble wine. Do not forget that this wine is from Tuscany, a place that throughout time has best exemplified nobility. Good Vino Nobile is pure class and elegance. Made from Prugnolo (another larger version of the Sangiovese grape), this is a wine for pastas, light meats, and bean dishes.

Super Tuscan
These are wines made by either unapproved grapes (Cabernet, Merlot etc), unapproved winemaking methods (smaller, non traditional oak barrels), or an unapproved composition (using 100% Sangiovese). Since these wines break the

rules, they may only be labeled Vino da Tavola (Table Wine). This should not imply that they are inferior, when in fact some Super Tuscans can actually be better than DOCG wines from Tuscany. Super Tuscans can be either red or white; however the reds being more popular and usually better wine.

Dessert

Vin Santo

In Tuscany, Vin Santo is typically made with the white grapes Trebbiano, Malvasia, and Canaiolo. In Pomino DOC (Tuscany) they actually make a red Vin Santo using Sangiovese, Cabernet, Merlot, and Cabernet Franc. To make Vin Santo, the grapes are first dried hanging in bunches. The grapes are then put into *caratelli* (small barrels) with the *madre*. Madre is the wine left over from the previous year, which itself of course contains a little from the previous year and so on etc. The wine goes through an oxidation process, which gives Vin Santo its typical nutty flavor. Some Vin Santo wines are sweet and therefore best suited for dessert while others may be dry and better used as an aperitif. Great with biscotti.

NORTHEAST

FRIULI VENEZIA GIULIA

Whites	Reds	Dessert
Pinot Grigio	Refosco	Picolit
Tocai Friulano	Pignolo	Verduzzo
Riesling	Schioppettino	
Ribolla Gialla	Tazzelenghe	
	Cabernet	
	Cabernet Franc	
	Merlot	

Whites

Pinot Grigio
The most popular Italian white in the U.S.. Pinot Grigio in northern Italy is dry, crisp, and light bodied. Nutty and spicy, it is great as an aperitif and with appetizers.

Tocai Friulano
The word Tocai appears in many different countries with slight differences in spelling and complete differences in what the grapes actually are. Tocai from Friuli is fleshy, and minerally with high acidity. Hints of nutmeg, almonds as well as peach and pear are common. Excellent wine to go with Baccalà (codfish), as well as almost any other fish.

Riesling
You should know that I am a staunch advocate for Riesling. The best is of course from Germany, but Friuli turns out some pretty good ones. The Rieslings in Friuli are drier and crisper than German ones. Goes well with almost anything.

Ribolla Gialla
One of my favorites when made well. Hints of apple and lemon, subtle with excellent balance and high acidity. One of the best seafood wines period.

Reds

Refosco
This Friuli red exhibits grassy characteristics with a bitter dry finish. Deep colored and dense. Dark chocolate and plums are also typical. When made correctly, it can be very good.

Pignolo
Sometimes compared to Brunello, Pignolo wines are dense and dark. High tannins with bitter cherry, black fruits like blackberries and slightly spicy. Good match with Pasta.

Schioppettino
Also called Ribolla Nera (the black version of Ribolla Gialla), Schioppettino has Syrah characteristics and therefore is quite Rhône like. It is difficult to grow and very hard to ripen. If made well, it can be spicy, peppery with blackberry and raspberry hints and high acidity. Nice with roasted meats.

Tazzelenghe
In Friulian dialect, Tazzelenghe means "tongue cutter". Obviously, as the name implies, this red is highly acidic. Dark and deep, good Tazzelenghe is not easy to get in the States.

Cabernet, Merlot, and Cabernet Franc
These three international grape varieties are quite popular here, but they are made very differently. Here they are not as full bodied and have less fruit than California ones. Herbal hints, tobacco, and bell pepper are more common due to the cooler climate of Friuli.

Dessert

Picolit
A white floral grape that can be dry or sweet; the latter being the best. It has a honeyed nectar hint. It is usually blended with dry whites to add sweetness and character.

Verduzzo
May be bone dry or sweet. Better known for its sweet version, the Verduzzo grape has high acidity and lemony hints.

VENETO

Whites	**Reds**	**Sparkling**
Bianco di Custoza	Bardolino	Prosecco
Soave	Valpolicella	
	Amarone	
	Ripasso	

Dessert	**After Dinner**
Recioto di Soave	Grappa
Recioto di Gambellara	
Recioto della Valpolicella	
Vespaiola	

Whites

Bianco di Custoza
Usually a blend of either Garganega, Riesling, Tocai, Trebbiano, and Malvasia. Getting better every year, Bianco di Custoza is finally making a mark in the wine world. Typically offers soft hints of peach and lighter in body than other Veneto whites. Perfect as an aperitif or with snacks. Great with light fish.

Soave
Made form Garganega and Trebbiano grapes. Typically light to medium bodied. Citrus notes and nutty hints are common. More producers are making better Soave now than ever. Try it with light fish.

Reds

Bardolino
Made form Corvina, Rondinella, Molinara, and Negrara. Very similar to Valpolicella but not quite as good, Bardolino is usually lighter bodied. Also made in a Rosé version called Chiaretto.

Valpolicella
In the region's dialect, Valpolicella means "valley of the many cellars". Corvina, Molinara and Rondinella are used. Valpolicella Classico are the best ones. When done right, it is one of my favorite wines. Hints of cherry, almonds with high acidity, Valpolicellas are very dry. Great with pasta and tomato sauce, rabbit, squash, etc.

Amarone
This is one of the most amazing things in life period! Amarone literally means "big bitter". The full name is actually Recioto della Valpolicella Amarone. Recioto comes from the dialect word "recie" meaning ears. Traditionally, the side clusters of the grape bunches were picked. It was believed that they received the most sunlight and therefore were better. Corvina, Molinara, and Rondinella grapes are air dried on trays in ventilated rooms sometimes up to four months. The grapes lose about half their water content and shrivel up. The sugars and flavors become ultra intensified. Essentially, the wine is made by pressing semi raisins instead of just grapes. This process is called appassimento. When the wine ferments, the producer has two options. If he *does not* let it ferment all the way to complete dryness, then it is essentially a sweet dessert wine. This is labeled Recioto della Valpolicella. If the wine is fully fermented all the way to complete dryness then it is called Recioto della Valpolicella Amarone or just simply AMARONE. Even though it is vinified dry, it never really seems so. The first swirl and sniff might indicate that the wine is very fruity, maybe even sweet. Once you taste, you get a fruity sweetness that turns bitter sweet. Then arrives the explosion of taste. Bitter chocolate, cherries, bitter cherries, plums, almonds, and much more. The great thing about good Amarone is that it offers so much but somehow manages to put it all together harmoniously in a perfectly balanced package. In winemaking, balance is hard to achieve and Amarone makes that task even harder. Due to the lengthy and expensive process used in making it, the customer will pay a healthy amount for good Amarone. When buying Amarone, avoid the new style ones that are so exaggerated they really give Amarone a bad name. Please do yourself a favor and set aside a special occasion to drink traditional Amarone.

Ripasso
The word ripasso means to repass. It refers to the Valpolicella wine that is repassed through the Amarone skins and pulp from the prior batch. It picks up body and flavor. In short, Ripasso is like a junior Amarone or like a cross between Valpolicella and Amarone. It also comes at a much smaller price than Amarone. Ripasso is a steal.

Sparkling

Prosecco
This grape is used for producing one of Italy's most famous sparklers. Prosecco is the wine used in making the very popular Bellini cocktail. Bellini is a drink that consists of Prosecco and peach nectar, made famous at Harry's Bar in Venice. Prosecco is dry with hints of almond and citrus. Good Prosecco is well worth a try and in some cases much better than some $25 bottles of Champagne.

Dessert

Recioto di Soave
Made form Garganega and Trebbiano grapes, Recioto di Soave is made using the passito grapes from the appassimento process. These wines are honeyed, peachy, with apricot and almond hints, and just plain delicious.

Recioto di Gambellara
Very similar to the Recioto di Soave. This one however is even harder to find in the States.

Recioto della Valpolicella
As described earlier in the Amarone section, this wine is made by stopping the fermentation earlier before it completely reaches dry. It is the step prior to actual Amarone. It is Port like and considered a dessert wine. If the fermentation is carried out fully then it is dry and considered Amarone.

Vespaiola
This white grape has a very high sugar content. It produces one of my favorite dessert wines. When the grapes are dried, it can be blended with Tocai and Garganega to produce a luscious dessert wine that is rich and velvety. Soft hints of apricots, baked pears, honey, brown spice, hazelnut and even vanilla. The high sugar content is remarkably balanced by the grape's natural high level of acidity. Absolutely a must try.

After Dinner

Grappa
There are many after dinner drinks in the world and Italy has more than plenty. Some of the famous ones are: Limoncello, Amaro, Grappa, etc, etc. I only will discuss Grappa since it is made from grapes. This is meant to be a wine book, so whatever is linked to wine will be mentioned. Grappa is made from grape pomace. Pomace is the left over pulp, skins, seeds, and stems, which remains after the juice has been pressed out. Initially, Grappa was considered a by-product. Eventually, wineries made their own Grappa to make a little extra money. Winery Grappas are never anything special and are made to help pay the bills. There are however whole companies dedicated solely to the production of Grappa. They do not make wine or anything else. JUST GRAPPA. These are the ones whose products you should seek out and try. Veneto is the ultimate place for Grappa although it is made all over Italy. There are also Grappas infused with fruits, herbs, and even chamomile. It may take some getting used to, but Grappa (like many Italian aperitifs and after dinner drinks) is meant to aid in digestion.

TRENTINO ALTO-ADIGE

Whites	**Reds**	**Dessert**
Pinot Grigio	Lagrein	Vin Santo
	Teroldego	
	Marzemino	
	Schiava	

Whites

Pinot Grigio

Trentino, a region noted world wide for its apples, also turns out some great Pinot Grigio. The soils and climate are perfect for this grape to prosper. Typical tastes such as nuttiness and spice are present.

Reds

Lagrein

Thought to originate from the river by the same name. There are two kinds: Lagrein Dunkel and Lagrein Kretzer (Rosé). The Lagrein Dunkel is dark with grassy hints, chocolate and plum characteristics. Lagrein is a grape with pretty good acidity and a low level of mild tannins. Lagrein Kretzer is the rosé version.

Teroldego

Mostly produced in the Rotaliano plain. Teroldego is a grape that makes medium bodied wines with grassiness, licorice and plum notes. Nice with hams and pasta with cream sauces.

Marzemino

This grape is thought to be related to Teroldego. Very similar characteristics. There is also a grape called Rebo, which is a cross between Marzemino and Merlot.

Schiava

This grape's name is derived from the Italian word for slave. What is the meaning? Who knows?!? Schiava is barely red, with hints of strawberry and even bacon. A light wine perfect for appetizers.

Dessert

Vin Santo

Here in Trentino, Vin Santo is made with the Nosiola grape. Not as good as Tuscan or Umbrian Vin Santo, but it is good with its crisp acidity and lightness. It is very hard to find this Trentino Vin Santo.

CENTRAL

MARCHE

Whites	**Reds**
Verdicchio	Rosso Conero
	Rosso Piceno

Whites

Verdicchio
The name of this grape derives from the Italian word for green, which is *verde*. It is verde because the grapes remain very green in color even when fully ripe. This grape makes wine with a resiny feel and pineapple hint. It also exhibits green herbs, anise, Bosc pears and green apples. This highly acidic grape is best known when producing wines in and around the city of Jesi. Look for Verdicchio dei Castelli di Jesi. Great with shellfish and obviously pasta with shellfish.

Reds

Rosso Conero
Considered to be Marche's best red. Made from at least 85% Montepulciano and a maximum of 15% Sangiovese. These wines have high acidity and deep cherry fruit. Great with chicken dishes and of course pasta of many kinds.

Rosso Piceno
Usually half Montepulciano/half Sangiovese. This wine comes off as a softer and fruitier Chianti. Can be a good simple value.

LAZIO

Whites	**Reds**
Frascati	Cabernet
	Merlot
	Shiraz

Whites

Frascati
A DOC zone that uses Malvasia, Trebbiano, and Greco. Very light, dry and crisp. Should be drunk carefree, as it is wine of little importance. Essentially, a thirst quencher.

Reds

Cabernet / Merlot / Shiraz
The soils here are perfect for international varieties such as these three. Lazio does better with these than their own indigenous grapes. On the southern coast of Lazio, the soils are great for Syrah which can tolerate heat and does not overproduce even in these fertile soils.

UMBRIA

<u>**Whites**</u>   <u>**Reds**</u>

Orvieto   Sagrantino di Montefalco
                                                          Montefalco Rosso

<u>Whites</u>

<u>Orvieto</u>
A DOC zone that produces wine made from Trebbiano, Malvasia, Grechetto and Verdello. Similar to Lazio's Frascati, but much better. Great as an aperitif wine and also with appetizers and light meats such as chicken.

<u>Reds</u>

<u>Sagrantino di Montefalco</u>
From the DOC zone of Montefalco, this wine is made with the Sagrantino grape. Very deep in color and very tannic. It is believed to be the most tannic grape in Italy and maybe the world. Too much tannin can be rough on the palate, but Sagrantino's tannins are surprisingly sweet in proportion to its high amount. It offers smokiness with bitter cherry hints. Great with pasta and truffles. Also great with an array of pork products and dishes.

<u>Montefalco Rosso</u>
A wine made with Sagrantino and Sangiovese. Not as exciting as straight Sagrantino, this wine can also be made using the appassimento process.

ABRUZZO

<u>**Whites**</u>   <u>**Reds**</u>

Trebbiano d'Abruzzo   Montepulciano d'Abruzzo

<u>Whites</u>

<u>Trebbiano d'Abruzzo</u>
A white grape that produces high yields. Very simple, dry and crisp. Nothing special.

<u>Reds</u>

<u>Montepulciano d'Abruzzo</u>
The grape is Montepulciano. This is not to be confused with Vino Nobile di Montepulciano, which is a Tuscan wine from the town named Montepulciano. In Abruzzo, the Montepulciano grape is very popular. Typically, Montepulciano is very fruity and quite simple. It is generally added in blends to add fruit and spiciness.

MOLISE

Reds
Montepulciano

Montepulciano
Molise is a small region that borrows a lot of its wine culture from neighboring regions. The Montepulciano grape seems to work best for this region. The style of the wine is strikingly similar to that made in Abruzzo. At one point, these two regions were collectively known as The Abruzzi.

SOUTH

CAMPANIA

Whites	Reds
Greco di Tufo	Taurasi
Fiano di Avellino	
Falanghina	

Whites

Greco di Tufo
Greco is a white grape grown all over the south of Italy but is most comfortable in Campania, specifically in and around a small town named Tufo. If made correctly, Greco di Tufo can be stunning. Nutty, slightly smoky, with soft hints of fruit. This wine graciously boasts high acidity. Perfect with almost any kind of fish and shellfish. Great with light white meats. Perfect for appetizers.

Fiano di Avellino
Fiano is a white grape that is aromatic, flowery, spicy and slightly honeyed. Its nuttiness is complimented by its typical peach characteristics. Very good with fish. Highly regarded to be Campania's best, I believe it is second to good Greco di Tufo.

Falanghina
Considered to be in between Greco and Fiano taste wise. It has high acidity like Greco and a fruit profile similar to that of Fiano.

Reds

Taurasi
Made primarily from the Aglianico grape. Taurasi is the purest and best expression of this grape. It can be blended with little amounts of Piedirosso, Sangiovese and Barbera. It has high acidity with dark berry fruits and a full bodied smoky feel. It is nicknamed "The Barolo of the South". Very austere in its youth, Taurasi gets better with age. Perfect for lamb or heavy pasta dishes.

BASILICATA

Reds

Aglianico del Vulture

Aglianico del Vulture
Hailing from Vulture (an extinct volcano), this Aglianico based wine is similar to that of Taurasi. Its structure is even bolder and it is more austere than Taurasi. Aglianico del Vulture also benefits from long ageing.

CALABRIA

### Reds	### Dessert
Cirò	Montonico
	Greco di Bianco

Reds

Cirò
A very unique wine made from an obscure grape called Gaglioppo. It produces unusual wines. Gaglioppo is light colored with hints of dried citrus, figs, and bitter chocolate. It has high alcohol and high acidity. Great with the famed pork products of the region.

Dessert

Montonico
A rare white grape that produces excellent dessert wines. Soft and elegant, Montonico produces wines that subtly offer hints of apricots, apples, oranges and even lemon rinds. Hard to find but worth the find.

Greco di Bianco
The famous Greco grape makes its appearance as a dessert wine here in the seaside town of Bianco. The grapes are semi-dried, so the flavors and high levels of sugars are concentrated. Very hard to find in the States.

PUGLIA

### Whites	### Reds
Locorotondo	Salice Salentino
	Primitivo di Manduria
	Uva di Troia

Whites

Locorotondo
Made primarily from the Verdeca grape. Nothing exciting, but definitely a summer sipping wine. It is light, high acid, with hints of apricots and nuts.

Reds

Salice Salentino
This DOC area makes wine produced primarily with the Negroamaro grape. Negroamaro translates to "black bitter". It might be an acquired taste, but Salice Salentino is a very dark and deep wine. It is highly tannic with hints of dark bitter chocolate and even licorice. Great with green vegetables and various pasta dishes.

Primitivo di Manduria
Primitivo is believed by many to be the ancestor of California's Zinfandel grape. Very similar fruit profile only better balanced. Primitivo has a higher level of acidity with a slightly lower level of fruit. High alcohol with bold dark fruits, Primitivo is a great wine with red meats and heavy pasta dishes.

Uva di Troia
A red grape that is deep colored with high alcohol. It makes concentrated wines that are rich and capable of ageing. Also blended to add depth and color. A wine more suitable for red meats.

THE ISLANDS

SICILIA

Whites	Reds	Dessert
Inzolia	Nero D'Avola	Moscato di Pantelleria
Carricante	Cerasuolo di Vittoria	Marsala
	Etna Rosso	Malvasia delle Lipari

Whites

Inzolia
Inzolia is typically blended with Trebbiano and Catarratto to form a fresh and lively white with exotic fruit flavors. Good match with seafood. Inzolia is also blended with Grillo to make Marsala.

Carricante
Mostly made on Etna, Carricante has hints of apples, oranges and anise. It has very good structure and is actually age worthy. A very hard wine to find but very unique and can be quite amazing.

Reds

Nero D'Avola
This is THE grape of Sicily. It is dark, soft and quite fruity. It has hints of dark cherries, plums, and blackberries. It can resemble Australian Shiraz, but actually is way better. This grape has high potential if made correctly. Great wine for meat dishes and pasta dishes.

Cerasuolo di Vittoria
Made primarily from Frappato and Nero D'Avola grapes. Frappato is a soft and low tannin grape with clear hints of strawberries and cherries. It is blended with Nero D'Avola for extra body and fruit.

Etna Rosso

The main grape here is Nerello Mascalese with smaller amounts of Nerello Cappuccio. The Mascalese variety is dark, spicy and high in alcohol. Etna red wines are also great with roasted meats.

Dessert

Moscato di Pantelleria

Sometimes the grapes are dried to produce a very sweet wine. Here the Moscato is called Zibibbo. Hints of apricots and peaches prevail.

Marsala

Similar to Sherry and Madeira, Marsala can be made dry, semi-sweet, or sweet. Marsala can be either made with white grapes (Inzolia, Cataratto, Grillo, Damaschino) or from red grapes (Perricone, Calabrese—a.k.a. Nero D'Avola, Nerello).

Malvasia delle Lipari

Malvasia is all over Italy, but is very well known to produce great apricot and peach scented sweet wine here in Lipari (an island off the coast of Sicily).

SARDEGNA

Whites	Reds	Dessert
Vermentino	Cannonau	Vernaccia di Oristano
Nuragus	Monica	
Torbato		

Whites

Vermentino

Floral, nutty, herbal and peachy. Very good in Sardegna and not as herbal as the Vermentino made in Liguria. It has high acidity and matches well with grilled fish.

Nuragus

A light white with nothing of much interest. Good for sipping or with snacks.

Torbato

Almost faced extinction (like many Italian grapes) but was rescued. Makes dry medium bodied wines. Highly regarded and worth it if you can find it.

Reds

Cannonau

The Sardinian name for Grenache. Here it provides powerful alcohol levels with ripe flavors and hints of earthiness. Full bodied and very fruity. Blackberries, coffee and pepper are also noted. Great with hearty meals involving meats such as roasted pork or lamb.

Monica

Sometimes this wine is compared to Syrah. Monica has lots of fruit including dark plums and black cherries. It can be smoky, earthy and above all spicy. It has relatively low tannins and low acidity.

Dessert

Vernaccia di Oristano

This is not to be confused with the Vernaccia of Tuscany. The Oristano version produces a wine similar to dry aged Oloroso Sherry. The grapes are picked very ripe and are extremely rich in sugar.

* Albany
1) Cayuga Lake
2) Hudson River Region
3) Long Island

NEW YORK

NEW YORK

BELIEVE it or not, but New York State is the U.S.'s second largest wine producing state (California is #1). New York does well with grapes such as Riesling and Chardonnay given its cool weather climate. It also plants Cabernet Sauvignon and Pinot Noir for red. The wines can be quite good but are usually quite expensive.

New York State has 3 main wine areas:

Long Island
Hudson River Region
Finger Lakes

The Finger Lakes is the state's most important wine region,
along with its sub zone Cayuga Lake.
Long Island is divided into North Fork and The Hamptons.

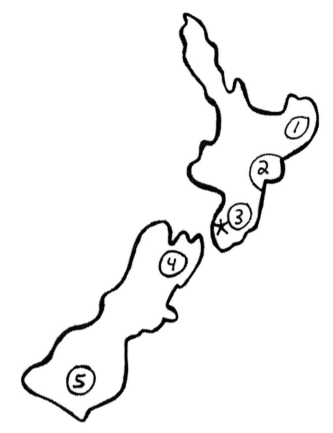

*Wellington
1) Gisborne
2) Hawke's Bay
3) Martinborough
4) Marlborough
5) Central Otago

NEW ZEALAND

NEW ZEALAND

OF all the New World wine countries; I pick New Zealand as my favorite. The whites are considered to be some of the top in the New World. The cool weather climate is perfect for the white Sauvignon Blanc grape. Pinot Noir also happens to do pretty well here. The wines are rarely oaked and the flavors are usually fresh while maintaining the all important high level of acidity. New Zealand wines can be a little fruitier than Old World wines, but never as exaggerated as those from California, South America, or even Australia. New Zealand is getting started early on what will soon take hold in the wine industry. Their aim is to use screw caps instead of corks. However the wines come packaged, New Zealand whites are excellent and you should make sure to try some.

The reds New Zealand produces are typically Pinot Noir and Cabernet. The Pinot Noir can be excellent while the Cabernets usually display herbal hints, typical when grown in cool weather climates.

Sauvignon Blanc

If you are looking for Sauvignon Blanc, there is no shortage here. The top wine area for this grape is Marlborough. The wines have the typical hints of herbs but also display exotic fruits as well a citrus. Can easily pair with most vegetables, even the impossible asparagus and artichoke. Great with an array of fish. Try it with pasta with pesto.

Chardonnay

The two places for New Zealand Chardonnay are Hawke's Bay and Gisborne. The Chardonnays here can be some of the best of all New World whites. If they are oaked, it is done minimally. Higher acidity than anything from California. Great with shellfish and fish. A great white for cream based dishes.

Pinot Noir

The cool weather of both Martinborough and Central Otago is perfect for Burgundy's Pinot Noir grape. Very versatile wines that match great with chicken, pork and also veal.

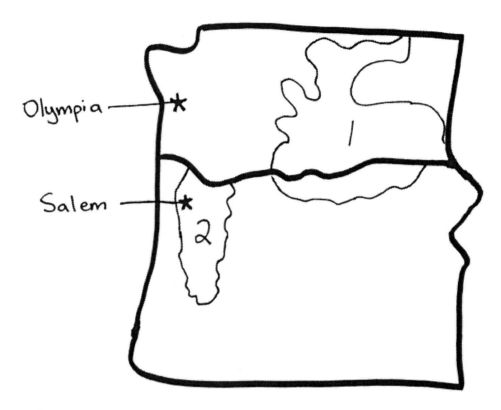

Olympia —— *

Salem —— *

1) Columbia Valley
2) Williamette Valley

OREGON
and
WASHINGTON

OREGON

PART of what is known as the Pacific Northwest, Oregon can produce really good Pinot Noir. It also makes good Pinot Gris, Riesling, and Chardonnay. The cool weather limits the variety of grapes that can be planted (and in this case, that's a good thing).

Oregon as well as Washington focus on only a few grapes and stick with them. Oregon rarely mimics California's tendency to follow trends. The main wine you will find from Oregon is red made from Pinot Noir.

Williamette Valley

THE place for Oregon Pinot Noir. The grape is hard to grow so expect to pay a substantial amount for good Pinot Noir. For $20 you can find a good bottle displaying hints of cherries and raspberries, strawberries and spice. The wines do have good acidity although some producers ruin it by ageing it too long in oak barrels. Great match with chicken, pork, turkey, and vegetable dishes.

WASHINGTON STATE

The other portion of the Pacific Northwest, Washington has even cooler weather than Oregon. It produces mostly Chardonnay, Cabernet, and Merlot.

Columbia Valley is the main wine area with two sub regions:

Walla Walla Valley
Yakima Valley

The Merlots from Washington State are considered the best in the U.S.A. Yes that's right, better than California Merlots. Although New World in style, it is not as big, over ripe, and clumsy as California Merlot. Washington's Merlots are full bodied with better acidity than the ones from California and hence much better with food. The Cabernet Sauvignons can also be very good and are much better with food than California wines.

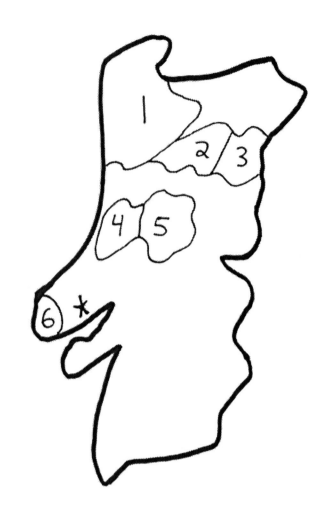

★ Lisbon
1) Vinho Verde
2) Douro
3) Port
4) Bairrada
5) Dao
6) Colares

PORTUGAL

PORTUGAL

QUICK, what's the first thing that comes to mind when you think Portuguese wine? Most likely you would answer Port. Port definitely is this country's most famous product, but Portugal also produces red and white wine. For very long, if it wasn't Port, nobody cared. But now people are starting to care. Portugal, like most European countries, is drowned in tradition. This can be a double-edged sword. Old ways of doing things has left Portugal's wine quality in the dark. Producers are starting to realize what works best for certain grapes to make certain wines. Newer, improved techniques are being used. Careful attention is being given to grape yields and vinification methods.

Portugal is planning to keep it smart. They are strong believers in using indigenous grapes to represent their country on the world wine stage. Red and white wines, in my opinion, will never replace the importance and quality of Port. Portugal *is* Port and will most likely remain so. It is their country's pride and joy. Portuguese wines go best with Portuguese food. The wines are simple and rustic like the food and people.

The better wine producing regions are located in the north.
The more important wine regions are broken down geographically as such:

NORTH	**CENTRAL**
Bairrada	Colares
Dao	
Douro	
Vinho Verde	
Port	

ISLAND

Madeira

NORTH

Bairrada

Bairrada produces mostly red wine made primarily from a grape called Baga. Smaller amounts of Periquita, Bastardo, and Tinta Pinheira are also included. The Bairrada reds are wines that need to age for quite a while. They have a lot of tannins and high acidity. Known as Portugal's top red wine region. Producers are trying to tame the rough tannins and soften the wine up as a whole. The newer wines are a little more fruit driven, but still considered big, tannic and acidic. The wine is well suited for red meat dishes.

Dao

Dao produces mostly red wine. They are very big and considered quite rough. These full bodied reds need time to soften. Quite popular wine region, although not on the same level of quality as the Bairrada wines. The main grapes are Alfrocheiro, Preto, Bastardo, and Touriga Nacional. The wines can be spicy with hints of forest fruits.

Douro

The Douro region actually has two major wine producing areas: Douro and Port. I have dedicated a section just for Port, but here I wish to discuss the reds and whites of just Douro. The reds and whites of the Douro are often pushed aside for the world popular Port. The reds are blends of Tinta Roriz (Tempranillo in Spain) and Touriga Nacional. For the whites, Verdelho is the main grape. Verdelho is believed to be the same as Spain's Godello grape.

Vinho Verde

Vinho Verde literally means green wine. The word green is meant to describe the wine's freshness and youthfulness, not its color. Vinho Verde can be red or white (the white being much, much better). The white Vinho Verde is made primarily from Alvarinho (Albariño in Spain). The wines are usually very dry and crisp (high acidity). They are also typically slightly effervescent. These qualities make Vinho Verde the perfect summer sipping wine. It is also great with shellfish and light snacks or as an aperitif.

Port

Portugal's most famous export is a sweet fortified wine. Ports may be white or red; however it is the red Port that conquers hearts and imaginations. The main grapes for red Port are Tinta Barocca, Tinta Cao, Tinta Roriz (Tempranillo in Spain), Touriga Nacional, and Touriga Francesa.

Halfway through the fermentation process, extra alcohol is added. This addition stops the fermentation process, leaving the wine with a lot of sugar that has not turned into alcohol. This extra sugar is called residual sugar. The result is a wine with a higher level of alcohol and sugar. The wine is then aged before its release. Port is one of the best options for after dinner. It is also a stunning match with blue cheeses like Roquefort or Gorgonzola. Some enjoy Port with fruits like strawberries. You will usually see some Ports with English names. Englishmen in Portugal created most of the Port companies and so named the companies after themselves.

There are many kinds of Port, but there are 3 main categories:

Ruby Port
Tawny Port
Vintage Port

Ruby Port

Ruby Ports are essentially Port wines made from lower quality batches. It is aged and then released. These are typically fruity with a light red color. Meant to be drunk young. Not considered anything great, so prices remain low.

Tawny Port

Tawny Ports are like the next step up (actually way, way up). They are made by combining blends of wines from different years. They are typically aged before release. They are called Tawny Ports because they are tawny in color. Cheaper Tawny Ports are sometimes made, which are essentially blends of White Port and Ruby Port. Forget this one and go straight for the Tawny Ports. These wines are sometimes aged 10, 20, 30, or even 40 years.

Vintage Port

The best and most expensive of all Ports. Only the grapes from a single vintage are used. These grapes are the best picks of all the batches and come from specially selected sites. It is also made only in the best vintages. A Port producer does not make Vintage Port every year. Remember, they must be from the best years or else there will be NO Vintage Port made. These Ports can age up to an astounding 50 years.

When I say "Vintage", it can be misleading. Vintage only denotes quality when it applies to Champagne or Port. These two wines use the word vintage to imply the wine from a certain year has been declared extraordinary and exceptional. In any other case, the word vintage is not meant to imply that the wine is either good or bad.

There are also a few kinds of Vintage Port:

Single-Quinta Port
Second Label Vintage Port
Late-Bottled Vintage Port
Colheita Port

Single-Quinta Port
A less intense Vintage Port with less fullness and richness.

Second Label Vintage Port
If a Port company does not feel that a vintage year should be declared, they bottle the wine as Second Label Port. The wines missed being declared completely Vintage but are of amazing quality nonetheless.

Late-Bottled Vintage Port
Made from the grapes of a single vintage (not a blend of different years) but the level of quality is not as high as the ones labeled simply Vintage. Also called LBV, it is considered like a high quality Ruby Port. Late bottled Vintage Ports cannot age as well as Vintage Ports. Drink early.

Colheita Port
Essentially the same as a Late-Bottled Vintage Port, but Colheita Port is aged longer considered to be more of a Tawny Port than a Ruby Port.

CENTRAL

Colares

Colares is mainly known for its red wine made from grapes like Ramisco, Periquita and Molar (among others). The wines are very tannic and need time to soften up. The full bodied wines of this area need ageing, as some people may find the amount of tannins excessive and unbearable.

ISLAND

Madeira

Forget the Madeira made in the States, which is a pathetic copy of the original. Real Madeira comes from the Island of Madeira. The wines are exposed to heat and oxidation. The resulting wines may be very dry to even sweet. Considered one of the top three fortified wines along with Port and Sherry.

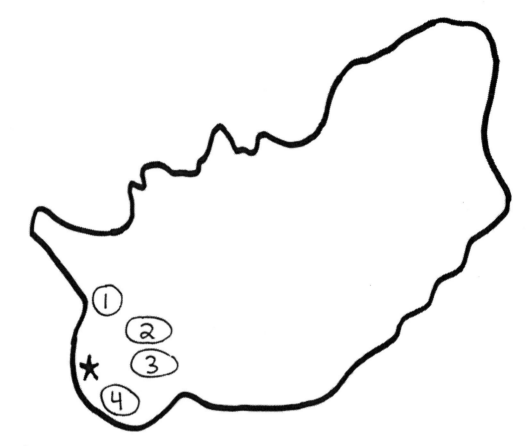

★ Capetown
1) Swartland
2) Paarl
3) Stellenbosch
4) Constantia

SOUTH AFRICA

SOUTH AFRICA

SOUTH Africa is up and coming. It makes reds and whites all from European grapes. Chardonnay, Sauvignon Blanc, Chenin Blanc, Cabernet, Merlot, and Shiraz are all planted here. The reds, however are what gain international attention. South Africa is famous for a grape called Pinotage. Pinotage is a cross between Pinot Noir and Cinsault, which the South Africans call Hermitage and thus the name Pinotage.

The main wine areas to know are:

Stellenbosch
Swartland
Constantia
Paarl

South African Merlots and Cabernets best represent this country on the world's wine stage. The abundant sunshine lets South Africa harvest ripe grapes full of fruit and body. The reds such as Shiraz, Cabernet and Merlot all go best with red meat.

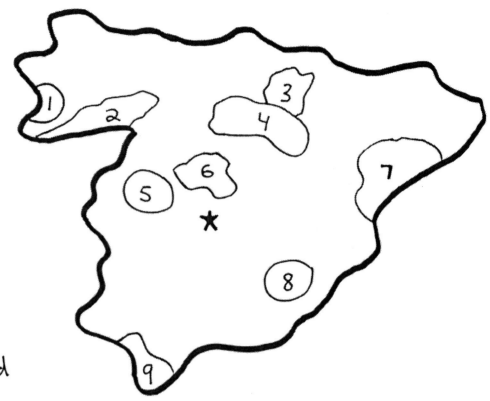

★ Madrid
1) Rias Biaxas
2) Ribeiro
3) Navarra
4) Rioja
5) Rueda
6) Ribera del Duero
7) Catalonia
8) Jumilla
9) Jerez

SPAIN

SPAIN

SPAIN has never been a country world renown for wine, although it plays a very important role in Spanish life. The image and reputation of Spanish wine is changing for the better. For long, Spain has been closely associated with Sherry, and pretty much nothing else. However; today, people are paying closer attention to newer, more exciting red and white wines coming out of Spain.

Spanish wine mirrors its culture, landscape, and people. Her wines are rustic and satisfying. The international varieties have invaded and taken over, but there are numerous good wines from indigenous grapes to be found. The international varieties seem to do very well when blended with Spain's indigenous grapes. Cabernet Sauvignon is typically blended with Spain's red Tempranillo grape. The results can be excellent.

I must mention that in Spain (as everywhere else) there are a few rotten apples. Some producers feel the urgent need to make new fashionable style wines. The result is a bunch of Spanish wines that all taste alike. Overoaked, overripe, and over everything for that matter. These wines should be overlooked. Some producers are trying too hard to conform to new wine trends. We could all send a message to these people by not buying their wines. They will then be forced to make better (real), more food friendly wine. Spanish wine goes best with Spanish food. This combination should not be sacrificed for the sake of jumping on the bandwagon.

This is not to say that the bulk of bad Spanish wine is the fault of those wannabe groupie wine producers. Spanish wine in general was suffering for a while. Rules and regulations were lax and people seemed not to care. Many Spanish grapes are only capable of producing ordinary, low acid wines with excessively high alcohol and no balance. Smart producers are now paying close attention to how to maximize the potential of Spanish wine and emphasize the grape's positive features rather than its flaws.

There are many wine producing regions in Spain.
The main 9 you should know are divided geographically.

NORTHWEST	**NORTH**	**NORTHEAST**
Rias Biaxas	Navarra	Catalonia
Ribeiro	Rioja	
	Ribera del Duero	
	Rueda	

SOUTHWEST	**SOUTHEAST**
Jerez	Jumilla

NORTHWEST

Rias Biaxas

Whites

Albariño

Albariño
This white grape is very thick skinned and therefore produces very little juice. The resulting juice is usually of very good quality. It is very aromatic and compared to Viognier and Gewurztraminer. It is lighter than the two with hints of peaches, apricots and its trademark characteristic of citrus. It has good acidity and is therefore food friendly. Good Albariño can be expensive, but worth the money. Perfect for shellfish, fish, white meats, appetizers, and even as an aperitif.

Ribeiro

Whites

Palomino
Godello

Palomino
Possibly one of the most worthless grapes for producing wine, in this case white wines. Totally a waste of time, UNLESS it is planted much further south where it is used to make the famous and stunning Sherries of the world. Unfortunately, here in the northwest, it is the most planted junk around. Fortunately, producers are realizing it is only good for Sherry and are planting the much, much better Godello.

Godello
Northwest Spain is waking up to Godello. What a relief! And it is about time. Producers are ripping out those crappy Palomino vines and are now planting Godello. Godello has nice hints of apricots and peaches. Not as good as Albariño, but close. These wines are compared to Portugal's Vinho Verde.

NORTH

Navarra

Rosado
Navarra is a wine region noted for nothing great except its great rosé wines. These rosés are typically made from Garnacha (Grenache in French) grapes and Tempranillo. I have tried some Rosados that are great and very inexpensive. You can do no wrong with these wines. They exemplify the word value.

Rioja

Rioja has long represented the epitome of Spanish wine. It is Spain at its core. Riojas have taken their place on the world stage and rightfully so. Rioja *is* red wine. The whites are mediocre at best. The main red grape is Tempranillo.

Smaller amounts of Garnacha, Carignan, and Graciano may be added. Tempranillo can be medium to full bodied with hints of strawberries, raspberries, black berries, black cherries and of course tobacco. Better drunk early. Great with pork and pork products. Match Rioja with poultry and other light meats.

Ribera del Duero

Ribera del Duero is proving to be a top contender as one of Spain's top reds (the whites are insignificant). The red grape most widely used is Tempranillo. The Tempranillos here differ from the Riojas in the sense that they are darker and more age worthy. As Ribera del Duero wines age, they exhibit dark plums and prunes. Bitter chocolate and of course tobacco are also present. These wines are typically quite rough. Drink Riojas earlier and save the Ribera del Dueros for later.

Rueda

The only wine region in northern Spain that makes really good white wine. Reds are nothing of importance. Rueda wines primarily blend white grapes such as Verdejo and Viura. The international white grape Sauvignon Blanc does exceptionally well here. Rueda wines can have hints of pears and grapefruit. If Sauvignon Blanc is added, then Ruedas become more exciting with better acidity and hints of dried herbs. Great wine for fish.

NORTHEAST

Catalonia

Catalonia has many wine producing areas.
The main 2 you should know are:

Penèdes
Priorato

Penèdes
Penèdes makes mostly white wine. Its whites are usually blends of grapes such as Parellada, Macabeo and Xarel-lo. Chardonnay has now become very popular in Penèdes and is used in the blends. The whites are pretty average and should be drunk as young as possible. These whites are also made into Cava, which is Spain's answer to Champagne. This Spanish sparkler is produced all over the north of Spain, but mostly concentrated in Penèdes, specifically the area of Cava. Cava Sparklers are never really anything special. The Penèdes region produces small amounts of red wine primarily from Garnacha. The international variety Cabernet Sauvignon can actually produce Penèdes' best red.

Priorato
Priorato is known strictly for its red wine, which is considered one of the best in Spain. Prioratos are hard to come by and quite expensive. It rushed onto the world's wine stage and it looks like it is here to stay (and that's a good thing). The main grape is Garnacha. Older Prioratos were very big, black, and alcoholic. They aged forever and were ready for consumption years after its release. New producers are making these wines a little more accessible. They may even blend Cabernet Sauvignon or Merlot. Priorato reds can have hints of black cherries, figs, spice, tar, and even leather. The alcohol is very high. Priorato is meant to go with red meat.

SOUTHWEST

Jerez

The motherland of Sherry. Sherry is a fortified wine made primarily from the white Palomino grape. There are 2 kinds of Sherry: Fino and Oloroso. The difference between the two is something called *flor*. Flor is a kind of yeast that is naturally present ONLY in Fino Sherries. Fino Sherry is lower in alcohol and therefore allows the flor to develop. Oloroso Sherry is too high in alcohol to allow flor to develop. The Sherry is aged in wood barrels but only filled about 80%. The other 20% gives room for the flor to develop (only in Fino Sherries). The flor eliminates exposure to oxygen and therefore prevents oxidation. The flor is what gives Fino Sherries their tangy and pungent characteristics. Fino does not age well. When it does age, it loses its flor. The Sherry then changes into an amber color and starts to taste a little nutty (similar to Oloroso).

This is labeled a Fino Amontillado. If the Sherry is aged longer and is softer and darker, it is then labeled simply Amontillado. Of all the Fino style Sherries the lightest and most pungent of all is called Manzanilla. Fino Sherries are considered to be the best of all Sherries.

Oloroso Sherry does not use and develop the flor. Without flor, Oloroso Sherry is prone to oxidation. This exposure to air is what gives Oloroso Sherry its characteristic dark brown color and nutty/raisiny taste. Olorosos are aged longer and are pretty high in alcohol.

Oloroso Sherry is best served between 56 – 60 degrees Fahrenheit.

Fino Sherries can be served chilled between 48 – 52 degrees Fahrenheit.

SOUTHEAST

Jumilla

Jumilla is an up and coming wine region. It historically produced average wines that were unbearably high in alcohol. New producers are now picking the grapes earlier to avoid high sugar content and therefore high alcohol. The main grape is Monastrell. Monastrell is the Spanish name for Mourvèdre. The wine is blended occasionally with small amounts of Tempranillo or Garnacha. International varieties like Cabernet Sauvignon and Merlot are also now being added. High in alcohol and low in acid, Jumilla wines have typical hints of blackberries and spice.

MATCHING WINE WITH FOOD

THE age old trick has always been white with fish and red with meat. While that may be true, it gets much more complicated than that. Nowadays, some people believe you should drink whatever you like with whatever you eat. You can do that, but you would be making more than a few mistakes. You are entitled to drink whatever you choose, but remember there are undeniable matches and mismatches when it comes to food and wine. Before getting into it a little more specifically, I wish to offer a few helpful guidelines.

Pair Body Weights
Light bodied wines go best with lighter dishes. Heavy dishes go best with heavier wines. A plate of grilled chicken and mashed potatoes would be overshadowed if paired with the typically humongous Amarone. You would do better with a Chablis.

Yin and Yang
A good tip is to balance opposites or extremes. If you were eating something salty and spicy, then a nice juicy and sweeter Riesling would be appropriate. For a cream based dish, a nice acidic wine can help cut the richness.

Do the Same
If you are eating a peppery steak, a nice compliment would be the peppery and spicy Rhône wines or other Syrah based wines. If a dish consists of roasted herbs, an herbaceous Sauvignon Blanc would do the trick.

When in Rome, Do as the Romans do (LITERALLY)
When pairing wine with certain ethnic cuisines, make it a habit to pair a wine made in the same region where the food is popular. Nothing marries better than the famous goat cheese from the Loire and her equally famous Sancerre (Sauvignon Blanc). This regional food and regional wine combination is nowhere better exemplified than in Italy. The food and wine tradition is older, more extensive and closely linked than those of any other country.

SOME DO'S AND DON'TS

1) Wine with salad is almost always a no-no. The vinegar ruins everything. I usually take a break when eating my salad and just drink water.
2) Red wine can taste metallic with many kinds of fish. The only reds I would ever pair with fish are Pinot Noir and Beaujolais.
3) Salty foods cry for sweeter wines to create a harmonious balance.
4) The spicier the food, the lower alcohol the wine should have. High alcohol and spice together would create a hot taste in the mouth.
5) Tannic red wines need red meat and vice versa. The fat helps soften the tannins, while the tannins help tackle a big dish like steak.
6) Asian cuisines such as Thai, Vietnamese, and Indian use many different spices. The main wines to stick with are Riesling and Vouvray for whites and Beaujolais and Cabernet Franc for reds.

Here is a list of the most popular dishes in America and the wines to accompany them.

GENERAL APPETIZERS

Whites

Muscadet
Sancerre
Champagne
Vouvray
German Rieslings Kabinett
Moscato D'Asti
Franciacorta Sparkling
Pinot Grigio
Greco di Tufo
Orvieto

Reds

Pinot Noir
Beaujolais
Rioja

PASTA

Know which region the pasta dish is from and pair it with the region's own wines.
Of course you can always go outside the lines and experiment with other endless options.

Pasta with Pesto
Whites
Arneis
Sauvignon Blanc
Ribolla Gialla
Tocai Friulano
Greco di Tufo
Pigato
Vermentino

Pasta with Eggplant
Reds
Nero D'Avola
Cirò
Primitivo
Taurasi
Rosso Piceno

Pasta with Mushrooms
Reds
Chianti
Dolcetto
Barbera
Valpolicella
Cabernet Franc
Teroldego
Lagrein Dunkel

Pasta with Garlic and Oil
Whites	*Reds*
Greco di Tufo	Chianti
Falanghina	Valpolicella
Gavi	Dolcetto
	Barbera

Pasta with Pumpkin
Reds
Nero D'Avola
Ripasso
Valpolicella
Dolcetto
Salice Salentino

Pasta with Broccoli
Whites	*Reds*
Arneis	Salice Salentino
Fiano di Avellino	Primitivo
Greco di Tufo	Cirò
Soave	

Pasta and Beans
Reds
Chianti
Montepulciano d'Abruzzo
Vino Nobile di Montepulciano
Rosso Conero

Pasta with Tomato Sauce

Reds
Barbera
Nebbiolo d'Alba
Valpolicella
Ripasso
Chianti
Vino Nobile di Montepulciano
Salice Salentino
Aglianico

Pasta with Cream based Sauces

Whites
Tocai Friulano
Ribolla Gialla
Pinot Grigio
Soave
Gavi

Reds
Valpolicella
Chainti
Montepulciano d'Abruzzo

Lasagne and other stuffed Pastas

Reds
Nebbiolo D'Alba
Barbaresco
Barolo
Ripasso
Amarone
Refosco
Pignolo
Schioppettino
Rosso di Montalcino
Brunello di Montalcino
Super Tuscan
Vino Nobile di Montepulciano
Chianti
Taurasi
Aglianico del Vulture

Pasta with Meat Sauces

Reds
Nebbiolo D'Alba
Barbaresco
Barolo
Ripasso
Amarone
Refosco
Pignolo
Schioppettino
Rosso di Montalcino
Brunello di Montalcino
Super Tuscan
Vino Nobile di Montepulciano
Chianti
Taurasi
Aglianico del Vulture
Nero D'Avola
Salice Salentino
Cannonau

Pasta with Shellfish

Whites
Verdicchio
Arneis
Gavi
Vermentino
Prosecco
Greco di Tufo
Tocai Friulano
Ribolla Gialla
Pinot Grigio
Soave

Risotto alla Milanese

Whites
Tocai Friulano
Ribolla Gialla
Fiano di Avellino

Reds
Oltrepò Pavese
Valpolicella
Ripasso
Nebbiolo D'Alba

Risotto with Vegetables

Whites
Tocai Friulano
Ribolla Gialla
Arneis
Sauvignon Blanc

Reds
Pinot Noir
Valpolicella
Chianti

Risotto with Shellfish

Whites

Verdicchio

Arneis

Greco di Tufo

Falanghina

Prosecco

Soave

Tocai Friulano

Ribolla Gialla

PIZZA

Reds

Barbera

Dolcetto

Chianti

FISH

Light Fish
Such as: Flounder, Sole, Trout, Bass, Red Mullet, and Fluke etc.

Whites

New Zealand Sauvignon Blanc

Sancerre

Chablis

German Rieslings

Greco di Tufo

Fiano di Avellino

Falanghina

Prosecco

Tocai Friulano

Ribolla Gialla

Pinot Grigio

Gavi

Fatty Fish / Oily Fish
Such as: Salmon, Blue Fish, Tuna, Swordfish, and Mackarel etc.

Whites	*Reds*
Meursault	Pinot Noir
Montrachet	
Chablis	
Alsace Rieslings	
Alsace Gewurztraminer	
Gruner Veltliner	
Viognier	
Albariño	

Sushi and Sashimi

Whites
German Riesling

Seafood Teriyaki

Whites
Spatlese Riesling
Vouvray

Salmon Teriyaki

Whites
Champagne
Prosecco

Shellfish

Whites
Verdicchio
Soave
Ribolla Gialla
Tocai Friualno
Pinot Grigio
Greco di Tufo
Falanghina
Albariño
Vinho Verde
Vouvray
German Riesling
Gruner Veltliner
Prosecco
Champagne

Ceviche

Whites
Prosecco
Champagne

Smoked Fish / Caviar

Champagne with these two is not
nearly the perfect match. Cold vodka
is your best choice.

CHICKEN, TURKEY, RABBIT, DUCK AND GOOSE

Rotisserie Chicken

Whites	*Reds*
Sauvignon Blanc	Pinot Noir
California Chardonnay	Cabernet Franc
	Rioja

Grilled Chicken

Whites
Alsace Riesling
Greco di Tufo

Chicken Cutlet

Whites	*Reds*
Tocai Friulano	Barbera
Pinot Grigio	Nero D'Avola

Chicken Teriyaki

Reds
Beaujolais
Cabernet Franc

Mole Poblano (Mexican Chicken Dish)
Reds
Côtes du Rhône
Cabernet Franc

Chicken Szechuan

Whites	*Reds*
Moscato D'Asti	Beaujolais
German Riesling Spatlese	Cabernet Franc

Barbecued Chicken
Reds
Chilean Cabernet

Fried Chicken

Whites	*Reds*
New Zealand Sauvignon Blanc	Chilean Cabernet
California Chardonnay	

Chicken Vindaloo (Indian)
Whites
German Rieslings
Gewurztraminer Vouvray
Gruner Veltliner

Chicken Saag (Indian)

Whites	*Reds*
Sauvignon Blanc	Rioja

Thanksgiving Turkey

Whites	*Reds*
Viognier	Zinfandel
German Riesling	Ripasso

Braised Rabbit
Reds
Valpolicella
Salice Salentino
Burgundy Pinot Noir
Oregon Pinot Noir

Duck/Goose Foie Gras
Whites
German Riesling (Kabinett or Spatlese)
Alsace Pinot Gris
Sauternes

PORK

Pork Chops
Whites
German Riesling
Alsace Riesling
Alsace Pinot Gris
Alsace Gewurztraminer
Gruner Veltliner

Braciola (Italian Pork Roulade)
Reds
Valpolicella
Ripasso
Nebbiolo D'Alba
Barbaresco
Cirò
Taurasi
Nero D'Avola
Etna Rosso

Charcuterie

Whites	*Reds*
Sancerre	German Pinot Noir
Greco di Tufo	Cabernet Franc
Gruner Veltliner	

Choucroute Garni

Whites	*Reds*
Alsace Pinot Gris	German Pinot Noir
Gewurztraminer	Rioja
Gruner Veltliner	

Barbecued Pork Ribs
Reds
Australian Shiraz
Chilean Cabernet

Ham

Rosé	*Reds*
Rosé d'Anjou	German Pinot Noir
Navarro Rosado	Lagrein Dunkel
Lagrein Kretzer	

Sausage

Whites	*Reds*
Greco di Tufo	Côtes du Rhône
Gewurztraminer	Australian Shiraz
Gruner Veltliner	Nemea
Albariño	Rioja
	Primitivo

Salami
Reds
Montepulciano d'Abruzzo
Cirò
German Pinot Noir

Cured Pork Products
Such as: Prosciutto, Mortadella, Speck, etc.

Whites	*Reds*
Tocai Friulano	German Pinot Noir
Ribolla Gialla	Lambrusco
German Riesling	Oltrepò Pavese
Gruner Veltliner	

LAMB

Rack of Lamb
Reds
Châteauneuf-du-Pape
Hermitage
Gigondas
Pomerol
Brunello di Montalcino
Rosso di Montalcino
Vino Nobile di Montepulciano
Barolo
Barbaresco
Washington State Merlot

Lamb Kebab
Reds
Nemea
Australian Shiraz
Salice Salentino
Faugères

Lamb Chops
Reds
Bordeaux
Priorato
Rioja

Lamb Vindaloo

Whites	*Reds*
German Riesling	Rioja
Gruner Veltliner	
Gewurztraminer	

Spit Roasted Lamb
Reds
Pomerol
Nemea
Salice Salentino
Washington State Merlot

Moussaka
Reds
Nemea
Côtes du Rhône
Cannonau
Nero D'Avola

BEEF, VEAL, BOAR, VENISON

Steak
Reds
Bordeaux
Hermitage
Cahors
Madiran
Barolo
Brunello di Montalcino
Pignolo
California Cabernet

Chateau Briand
Reds
Côte-Rôtie
Châteauneuf-du-Pape
Amarone
Refosco
Schioppettino
Australian Shiraz
California Zinfandel

Pot Roast
Reds
California Cabernet
Australian Shiraz

Meatloaf
Reds
California Cabernet
Australian Shiraz

Chili con Carne
Reds
Côtes du Rhône
Australian Shiraz
Chilean Cabernet
Primitivo

Hamburgers
Reds
Australian Shiraz
California Cabernet
Chilean Cabernet
Primitivo

Osso Buco (Veal)
Reds
Chianti Riserva
Super Tuscan
Refosco
Barolo
Barbaresco

Veal Scaloppine Piccata
Whites
Tocai Friulano
Ribolla Gialla
Greco di Tufo

Veal Marsala
Whites
Greco di Tufo
Tocai Friulano
Soave

Reds
Pinot Noir
Chianti
Valpolicella
Etna Rosso
Nero D'Avola
Dry Marsala

Bresaola (Italian Air Dried Beef)
Carpaccio (Raw Sliced Beef)
Steak Tartare
Reds
Oltrepò Pavese
Refosco
Pignolo
Barbaresco
Nebbiolo D'Alba
Rosso di Montalcino

CHEESE

Goat Cheese
Such as: Caprini, Montrachet, Boucheron, Chevre, Crottin de Chavignol
Whites
Sauvignon Blanc
(Particularly Sancerre)
Rich Double and Triple Cream Cheese
Such as: Pierre Robert, Explorateur, Sainte Andre

Champagne
Oloroso Sherry
Tokaji Aszù (Hungary)

Soft Ripened Cheese
Such as: Brie, Camembert

Whites	*Reds*
Champagne	Pinot Noir
	Beaujolais

Semi Soft Cheese
Such as: Gouda, Fontina, Emmenthal
Whites
Meurasult
Alsace Riesling
Ribolla Gialla
Tocai Friulano

Semi Hard Cheese
Such as: Cheddar, Kasseri, Mahon, Gruyere, Comte

Whites	*Reds*
Alsace Riesling	Rosso Piceno
Gewurztraminer	Montepulcinao d'Abruzzo
Gruner Veltliner	Nero D'Avola
Tokay D'Alsace (Pinot Gris)	Cannonau

Hard Cheese
Such as: Parmigiano, Asiago, Roncal, Aged Gouda

Please note that Parmigiano Reggiano is believed to be the most versatile cheese.
It can be matched with nearly every red and
does magnificent when matched with Champagne.

Whites	*Reds*
Champagne	Amarone
Prosecco	Ripasso
Ribolla Gialla	Barolo
Tocai Friulano	Barbaresco
	Nebbiolo D'Alba
	Brunello di Montalcino
	Rosso di Montalcino
	Vino Nobile di Montepulciano
	Super Tuscans
	Lambrusco
	Châteauneuf-du-Pape

Blue Cheese
Such as: Gorgonzola, Roquefort, Stilton, Cabrales

Port
Sauternes
Oloroso Sherry
Pear Liqueur
Recioto della Valpolicella
Amarone

DESSERT

I do not agree with pairing dessert with a sweet wine. The dessert is sweet enough and matching sugary desserts with a sugary drink is just too sugary. The tastes become masked and you cannot appreciate either the dessert or dessert wine. If you must match something with a dessert, try to get a dry wine to cut through the richness of the dessert. The only sweet wine I would probably ever pair with a dessert is Moscato D'Asti. Moscato can actually bring out the flavors of the dessert, but that is only if you must drink a dessert wine with your dessert.

RETAIL

THE best, and cheapest, way to discover wines is to buy them from a good wine store. Retail is the most inexpensive and legally possible way of purchasing wine. The only hard part is finding a good wine store. Before addressing the wine shop problem, let's first talk about prices. All wine stores buy from the same people (distributors). Sometimes, if the wine store buys a certain product in bulk, it costs less per case of wine and therefore a cheaper price is charged to the consumer.

There are many kinds of stores. You have the mega size stores that are practically wholesalers. They sell the *well known* brands at cheaper prices (at cost or sometimes even at a loss). This draws people in and is a great strategy if mass marketed wines are the theme of the store. The problem is that all other less known brands are marked up even higher to help pay for the money lost on the well known products. In short, mega stores offer values only on highly publicized wines that are usually not that great anyway. These mega stores are great if you need to buy a lot of liquor or wines with well known names. The negative, though, is that these stores are not always the place to find unknown wines that do not and cannot charge too high of a price. These wines can be unbelievable values. If the mega store does happen to stock such a wine, it will usually be marked up to an astronomical price. The other downside of mega stores is that you will have a 99% chance of not finding anyone who can really help you and has any knowledge on the subject of wine whatsoever. Most are staffed with college kids trying to make a few extra bucks. I do not dislike mega store. In fact, I appreciate them and thank them for helping to give a push to the local economy. I think mega stores are great for the purposes they serve.

The opposite of the mega store is a smaller, neighborhood store. You are not guaranteed to find great wines in a smaller store, but the probability is much higher than that of a mega store. Small stores operate on smaller budgets and cannot compete with huge stores on prices. This encourages the smart stores to direct their attention to lesser known wines that can be great values at low prices. These prices stay low because the wineries do not pay tons of money for advertising. The small store, if you are lucky, will more likely have a staff that is familiar with the wines and hopefully tastes them all before buying the wines.

A good wine store should have a well informed staff. This includes knowledge of wine and food pairing. The staff should always ask the customer what he or she is eating to better know which wine to offer. If the customer is not having the wine with dinner, the staff member should know which wines are great for situations that do not call for food. The staff member should offer the customer the best wine at whatever price he/she is willing to spend. A good wine store should also offer a vast selection of non oaked, non mass marketed wines.

While on the subject of retail, I must tell you all that the price situation does not seem to be getting better. This is usually *not even* the fault of the wine store. Every state has its own liquor laws, but not one stands tall as an example of consumer friendly. New York State for example is a miserable place when it comes to liquor laws. They are slowly changing some things around BUT those laws that intrude and increase prices seem to never go away.

Allow me to explain how wine gets from one place to the consumer. Let us take for example French wines. Egos and popularity already boost prices, but laws boost them even further. This is not just France, it is every wine country. The wine maker in France is faced with so many stupid laws and taxes that before it leaves the vineyard, it already costs more than it should. I must not fail to mention that if the winemaker faced a bad year, prices go up to pay for such an occurrence. I'm not just talking about money problems, I am referring to natural problems. If there was a hurricane or whatever, the prices go up.

For an American importer to bring in a wine to this country, he/she must first get a license. Of course there is no need to say that this license comes at a price. Then, when the importer buys the wine, he is paying all kinds of increases from exchange rates and of course more taxes on the actual sale. Now, an importer must sell the wine to a distributor who distributes it. An importer can also be a distributor, BUT distributing requires yet another license and yet another fee. Some companies have enough capital and are big enough to take on the distributing side, while others are either not that fortunate or simply do not even bother with the hassle. When an importer sells to a distributor, there is yet another tax imposed. All these taxes and I have yet to discuss the income taxes these people are doomed to face. Now, income tax does not really affect the consumer but I want you to get my point.

Anyway, I AM NOT FINISHED. The distributor must now sell to restaurants and retailers and guess what…another tax is imposed. Now the retailer and restaurants have to have their own license and that is another fee paid to that good ol' government. When the retailer or restaurant sells the wine to the consumer, there is the final sales tax. In the end, you the consumer gets screwed. If this bothers you as a consumer, then I suggest you change your voting habits.

This may shock some people, but the government probably makes more off a bottle of wine or liquor than whoever is involved with the actual making, importing, distributing, and selling of that product. Take for example full on socialist countries such as Canada. Canadian wines and liquors actually *cost more in Canada* than they do in the U.S.A.. A Canadian once told me that about 65% of a bottle's cost results from government imposed taxes. Maybe that is not an exact figure, but I would bet it is pretty close. This is absurd. Governments claim to raise taxes on such things as to prevent underage drinking. NOW, COME ON!!! We know that is a complete joke and so do the government officials who make up these laws. Look at the taxes on cigarettes. They are called "sin taxes". Cigarettes cost $8 a pack in 2004 in NYC. These taxes in no way prevent people from smoking. What they do though is cut job growth and productivity. This is a "sin".

RESTAURANTS

I am always sympathetic to the cries of businesses when they complain that things cost too much. I believe businesses should be allowed to freely operate with each other to offer the consumer the best price possible. While I understand the need for restaurants to make their money (and they should), I do feel that some simply take it to the next level. Too many restaurants mark up their wines exponentially. It is now the trend, in New York at least, to mark up a wine 400 – 500 %. The *fair* mark up is 250 – 300%, but this seems to be completely ignored. What restaurants do not understand is that by lowering their prices, a customer is more likely to buy 2 bottles at the fair price than just one at the inflated price. This is a simple law of doing business, but most restaurateurs do not care about business. They care about EGO.

Too many restaurants offer wine lists that are boring, long and expensive. I love wine BUT I do not feel like reading a 60 page wine list. The wine list is only so long for the simple reason that the restaurateur wants the consumer to be in awe of him and his restaurant. NEWS FLASH TO RESTAURATEURS….NOBODY CARES!!! What people care about is having fun at a restaurant with good food at affordable prices.

Of course, the ritzy incredibly high end restaurants can justifiably charge high prices for wines. Their clientele can easily afford it. The problem is that not every restaurant is on that level with that clientele. By raising wine prices, the regular restaurants are not changing the reality that their customers *simply do not want to pay such high prices*. They are also **not** elevating their status and catapulting their restaurants into that upper echelon. These hard headed restaurateurs usually go out of business and justifiably so.

A restaurant should offer wines that go with their food. Too many times, this is unfortunately not the case. The lists offer all these big names that may be good to great but do not compliment their food. These wines are there for purposes of showing off (again, the whole ego thing). A restaurant that takes wine seriously should have on hand someone who can help the customer choose the best wine that goes with the meal and is in the customer's budget. The restaurant should also offer wines by the glass that not only compliment the food but also hopefully offer the customer a chance at trying something new and exciting.

To the customer, I have only one thing to say. Please do not return a bottle just because it is not what you expected. Once the bottle is opened, you must pay for it. A bottle should only be returned if the wine went bad. The restaurant cannot keep opening wines (at their expense) until you find one you like. I know most people would never do such a thing, but there are those annoying few who feel it is their duty to make others blood boil.

INDEX

Printed in the United States
96197LV00002B/1-150/A

9 781589 611689